Wisdom

The Way to Human Flourishing

Darrow L. Miller

with Gary Brumbelow

Books by Darrow L. Miller

Servanthood: The Vocation of All Christians

Discipling Nations: The Power of Truth to Transform Cultures,
with Stan Guthrie

God's Remarkable Plan for the Nations,
with Scott Allen and Bob Moffitt

God's Unshakable Kingdom,
with Scott Allen and Bob Moffitt

The Worldview of the Kingdom of God,
with Scott Allen and Bob Moffitt

Against All Hope: Hope for Africa,
with Scott Allen and the African Working Group of
Samaritan Strategy Africa

On Earth As It Is in Heaven: Making It Happen,
with Bob Moffitt

The Forest in the Seed, with Scott Allen

*Nurturing the Nations: Reclaiming the Dignity of Women in
Building Healthy Cultures*,
with Stan Guthrie

LifeWork: A Biblical Theology for What you Do Every Day,
with Marit Newton

*Emancipating the World: A Christian Response to Radical Islam
and Fundamentalist Atheism*

Recovering Our Mission: Making the Invisible Kingdom Visible

Rethinking Social Justice: Redeeming Biblical Compassion,
with Scott Allen and Gary Brumbelow

Wisdom

The Way to Human Flourishing

Darrow L. Miller

with Gary Brumbelow

YWAM PUBLISHING
Seattle, Washington

YWAM Publishing is the publishing ministry of Youth With A Mission (YWAM), an international missionary organization of Christians from many denominations dedicated to presenting Jesus Christ to this generation. To this end, YWAM has focused its efforts in three main areas: (1) training and equipping believers for their part in fulfilling the Great Commission (Matthew 28:19), (2) personal evangelism, and (3) mercy ministry (medical and relief work). For a free catalog of books and materials, call (425) 771-1153 or (800) 922-2143. Visit us online at www.ywampublishing.com.

Wisdom, the Way to Human Flourishing
Copyright © 2019 by Darrow L. Miller

Published by YWAM Publishing
a ministry of Youth With A Mission
P.O. Box 55787, Seattle, WA 98155-0787

ISBN 978-1-57658-908-3 (paperback)
ISBN 978-1-57658-658-7 (e-book)

Library of Congress Cataloging-in-Publication Data — Pending

First printing 2019

Printed in the United States of America

To the Disciple Nations Alliance secretariat—
Scott Allen, Shawn Carson, Jessie Christensen,
Mary Kaech, and Dwight Vogt—
and the larger DNA global network

Contents

Introduction

Wisdom and Flourishing

Imagine a world where there is no corruption, only justice; no violence or conflict, only social peace; no wickedness, only goodness; no mediocrity, only excellence; no hideousness, only beauty; no greed, only generosity; no slavery or human trafficking, only freedom; no sickness, only health; no death, only life. Imagine a world where there is no poverty, only flourishing, a world where everyone is wise and no one foolish.

Does that sound like a real world to you? Does such a life sound at all normal? What would you say if I told you that I have just described exactly what God considers normal? What He has always intended for people? Would you laugh?

Yet this is exactly what God had in mind from the very beginning.

In the beginning God put Adam and Eve in paradise, a perfect place to live. Their experience is matched only by the imagination today. But even the notion of paradise does not fully capture Eden. Other religious and belief systems speak of a paradise concept. The Hindus have nirvana, for example. But the paradise of Eden was different. Eden was not simply a place to rest and dream. It was a place to make things happen. Eden was an environment in which humans were to flourish—that is, to thrive, expand, and prosper. But it was not only for their own flourishing; they were to bring flourishing to the creation around them. God had an assignment for the man and the woman in Eden, to take dominion over the creation. He gave them the mandate to begin with the raw materials of creation and develop it, make it flourish. They were to plant vineyards and orchards, domesticate animals, design irrigation systems, compose music and dance, invent technologies, build cities, navigate the seas, explore the cosmos. All this is part of human dominion, living as stewards of God's magnificent creation. These examples of agriculture and art and science are the ingredients of what we call culture. God mandated that humans would create culture.

Here's a related observation: God intended that humans flourish. Human poverty had no place in God's original design. In God's view (another way to say "in reality") all of life was to flourish. God wanted the human to develop in every dimension. Hebrew writers had a word for this: *shalom*, defined as completeness, soundness, welfare, peace.

That God should want whole-life flourishing for humans should not sound strange. It's the same thing earthly parents want for their children, wholeness in all dimensions of life: physical, social, spiritual, intellectual, emotional, financial, vocational. Why do human parents want these for their children? Because parents (as well as children) are made in God's image. Humans did not dream up these ideas on their own; they received them from God.

Human history began in a paradise. But not far into the story everything changed. Man rebelled.[1] As a result, man lost his place in the garden and the whole creation was marred. A cosmic reversal—theologians call it the fall—took place. Much of the original beauty was defaced. Glory was turned to shame, abundance to poverty, freedom to enslavement, order to disorder.

I (Gary) saw a little picture of this cosmic reversal some years ago. One August I traveled with three other people by car from Portland, Oregon, to Saskatchewan, Canada, a trip of about one thousand miles. On the way to Saskatchewan, the weather was very hot, as is normal for August. Our trip took us through southern Alberta, home to some of the best wheat farms anywhere. August is the month for harvest, so the crops were almost ready to take out of the field. And that year the crops were especially bountiful. After about four days in Saskatchewan we started back to Oregon, when something bizarre happened. A freak snow storm came through in the middle of the wheat harvest. The snow was very wet and heavy, and it destroyed much of the crop. We stopped in Lethbridge, Alberta, and went into a restaurant for lunch. A farmer was standing in line in front of us, talking to someone. With a heavy heart he said something that reminds me of this cosmic reversal: "One day I had the best wheat crop I've ever had. The next day it was all gone."

Ever since this cosmic reversal we have lived in a broken world. Nations, communities, lives are broken. But God's intentions have not changed. He wants individuals, communities, and nations to flourish. In fact, you could say that God is taking history back to where it began. Human history began in a garden paradise, and the end of history pictures a "city garden" and paradise restored. And God shares with humans the responsibility to create environments where people can flourish. I believe this is the best way to understand the creation mandate.

CREATED TO FLOURISH

In the creation account, God told the man and the woman, "Behold, I have given you every plant yielding seed that is on the face of all the earth, and every tree with seed in its fruit. You shall have them for food" (Gen. 1:29). Later, after the flood, He repeated the same statement to Noah and his family: "Every moving thing that lives shall be food for you. And as I gave you the green plants, I give you everything" (Gen. 9:3). God created humans who needed food to live, and he provided food for these needy humans.[2]

We typically think of dirt and seeds as so simple and ordinary as to be of interest only to farmers and gardeners. We rarely consider the power of the soil, or the potential of a seed. When a seed is put into the ground, it begins a multiplying process that is almost inconceivable. One seed produces an entire plant with many seeds—sometimes hundreds or thousands—each one of which has the power to repeat the cycle. God is the One who gives the growth to the plant, and He assigns humans dominion over this process for our nourishment and sustaining. Human dominion helps the creation to flourish. The God who created a flourishing universe made humans His agents in that flourishing process. If you are flourishing, you are bringing shalom to others because you are being what God intends you to be.

Earlier we pointed out that to flourish means to thrive, to expand, to prosper.[3] The word comes from the Hebrew *parah*, a verb variously translated as "sprout," "blossom," "flourish," "thrive."[4]

In God's original design, flourishing was the normal way of things. After the cosmic reversal, brokenness and withering—within human beings, their institutions, and in creation—became the new normal. Or to put it a little differently, the abnormal became the normal. Yet God has been working ever since to reset the creation. He is moving the creation from wasting away to flourishing, from poverty to prosperity, from disorder to order, from injustice to justice, from ignorance to knowledge, from sickness to health, from deformation to reformation.

So what does all this say about human responsibility for poverty and underdevelopment? How do we solve these problems? As a matter of fact, God has already equipped people to do that. He has provided the primary resource humans need for these solutions. What is that resource? Wisdom! Wisdom is what moves people from brokenness to wholeness, from poverty to flourishing, from underdevelopment to development. Wisdom is about life and governing in the time between paradise lost and paradise restored. Wisdom and human development, or human flourishing, are organically related. The second depends on the first. But not everyone understands that. That's why we wrote this book.

Many people working in government programs, and relief and development organizations, look largely to money and technology to solve poverty. Both money and technology can be part of the solution. But the solution to poverty lies much deeper. Relief and development workers need to see the connection between wisdom and human development.

Many people of faith care about the poor. They may be working with urban poor people in the United States, or in poor communities abroad. Many believe in a God who has revealed Himself to man. They believe in God's revelation, but they, too, have failed to make the connection between what that revelation says about wisdom, on the one hand, and the roots of poverty, on the other. People in both groups unknowingly operate from humanistic principles, policies, and programs. We are writing this book to address these gaps. We hope to show both kinds of people the connection between wisdom and human flourishing.

THE ROOT OF POVERTY

When I (Darrow) was a teen in California I traveled to Mexico City where I saw poverty for the first time. I was never the same. Within a few years I was working in an international relief and development organization. Like many of my peers, I was eager to help people break the ugly chains of poverty. Our organization, like many other such groups, spent lots of money in poor communities. The notion was that this money would help people move out of poverty. But I gradually realized we were operating with a fundamental misconception, namely, that poverty exists because of a lack of resources. People were poor because they lacked material resources. Not long into my career I came to realize how mistaken that view is. In fact, I recognized that it comes from Marxism: people are poor because they lack resources, and the solution lies in redistribution schemes. I came instead to see that the root of poverty is in the mind.

The human mind is a wonderful resource—perhaps the greatest created resource—and an asset for making a significant contribution to the individual and to society. On the other hand, the mind can be a liability. Many people live with mental strongholds that enslave them in poverty. One way we see this is how individuals relate to the creation order.

God created the universe in an orderly fashion, according to His own guiding principles. There is order in the universe and that order sustains our lives. Some people call this the creation order. People who are wise discover this order and live within its framework. When a person or nation lives within the framework of God's order, they tend to flourish. People who are foolish deny God, or His order, and try to live apart from it. To rebel against God's created order is to move toward poverty and enslavement.

The false idea that poverty is rooted in the lack of resources gives rise to redistribution schemes based on Marxist concepts. Poverty is grounded in the mind, not in the lack of resources. Underdevelopment is not *merely* a state of mind, but it is *sourced* in the mind. God has provided all the resources necessary for human flourishing. In the history of the world, one people in particular has demonstrated this.

THE INSIDE AND THE OUTSIDE

Several years ago I read a book by Thomas Cahill, *The Gift of the Jews: How a Tribe of Desert Nomads Changed the Way Everyone Thinks and Feels.* The book is the second volume in Cahill's Hinges of History series. He testifies that "in this series . . . I mean to retell the story of the Western world as the story of . . . those who entrusted to our keeping one or another of the singular treasures that make up the patrimony of the West."[5]

Through the life of Abraham, the world was introduced to monotheism. Cahill believes that Abraham, the father of the monotheistic faiths of the Jewish, Christian, and Muslim peoples, is one of the hinges of history. Before him, human society was dominated by an animistic/fatalistic culture. After him, everything changed.

> The Jews gave us a whole new vocabulary, a whole new Temple of the Spirit, an inner landscape of ideas and feelings that had never been known before. Over many centuries of trauma and suffering they came to believe in one God, the Creator of the universe, whose meaning underlies all his creation and who enters human history to

bring his purposes to pass. Because of their unique belief—monotheism—the Jews were able to give us the Great Whole, a unified universe that makes sense and that, because of its evident superiority as a worldview, completely overwhelms the warring and contradictory phenomena of polytheism. They gave us the Conscience of the West.[6]

Instead of a world in which every tribe had its own deity, now one could embrace the concept of one God who had created the universe. It was this understanding of monotheism that would eventually produce the Western world. Before Abraham, people lived their lives based on lies. The last reference to any meaningful relationship between God and man is Noah's blessing on his sons (Gen. 9:26–27) many generations in the past. No doubt oral stories of the creation, the flood, and the tower of Babel were being told. But the record between the flood in chapter 9 and the call of Abraham in chapter 12 suggests alienation between God and humans. In Ur, Abraham lived among pagans and was probably a pagan himself. The Jews brought truth to the world, including what Cahill calls "the Outside and the Inside." The outside is reality, the order of creation. The inside is the way of seeing—the worldview—that comports with reality. "The Jews gave us the Outside and the Inside—our outlook and our inner life. We can hardly get up in the morning or cross the street without being Jewish. We dream Jewish dreams and hope Jewish hopes. Most of our best words, in fact—new, adventure, surprise; unique, individual, person, vocation; time, history, future; freedom, progress, spirit; faith, hope, justice—are the gifts of the Jews."[7]

LIVING IN GOD'S CREATION ORDER

God's order is life-giving. When we discover His creation order and live within its framework, we are entering the environment God made for human flourishing. Individuals and nations tend to flourish when they live within God's creation order. But when they deny that order or foolishly choose to live outside it, poverty is the result. Instead of becoming all God intends us to be, we disintegrate—we become less than God's intentions. We see this in broken lives and broken communities all over the world. This is poverty!

Because I (Darrow) want to see poor individuals and nations come out of poverty, I have spent the last thirty years of my life studying the Bible to find out what it says about nations flourishing. A few years ago I began to study Proverbs. This is a very practical book, a book about how to live and work. Proverbs lays the groundwork for living. It is comprehensive; it speaks to every area of our lives and every sector of society. Proverbs is heaven's message for earth's living.

Among other things, Proverbs is about governance—the art of living and working. For our purposes, *governing* is distinguished from the *institutions of government*; we will return to that point shortly. Proverbs teaches us how to govern ourselves as individuals, as communities, and as nations. Governance is the means to flourishing. Proverbs not only identifies flourishing as the goal of life; it also prescribes the means to that goal. Flourishing—personal, community, and national development—begins by turning away from the voice of folly and turning toward the voice of wisdom.

Folly takes different forms, but surely one of the clearest expressions of it in today's societies has to do with efforts to redefine marriage and the family. Daniel Diaz was in a class where I lectured in Puerto Rico. Recently he returned to his home country of Argentina where he heard a senator say, "We are the best country in the world because we have five different classes of family: mother and father, single mother, single father, two mothers, two fathers!" When we lose sight of such a fundamental truth—God's creation of the man and the woman, of sex and marriage and families—we are foolish and will descend into brokenness and poverty.

Another dimension of human flourishing is freedom. Man was created to be free; enslavement and bondage had no place in God's intentions. With respect to freedom, Alexander Tocqueville wrote to his friend Eugene Stoffels, "To persuade men that respect for the laws of God and man is the best means of remaining free . . . you say, cannot be done. I too am tempted to think so. But the thing is true all the same, and I will try to say so at all costs."[8]

We pointed out that God gave the man and the woman the mandate to develop the earth. That creation mandate introduced the concept of human governance. God delegates authority; we are His stewards of creation, His vice-regents. These are governing concepts. And fundamental to this notion of governance—of our lives and of the creation—is something Proverbs has a lot to say about: work.

THE WORK OF GOVERNANCE, THE GOVERNANCE OF WORK

Proverbs tells us that our daily lives are about governing. For example, you are exercising governance when you go to work every day. My friend Christian Overman says our work is about governance. "*Work*, at its core, is an act of governance. Governance over wood, metal, cows, cotton, and carrots. Governance over sound waves, electrical currents, and wind. Governance over computer keyboards, fiber optics, and digital images. Governance over people. Governance over things. Governance over ideas."[9]

Earlier we pointed out that government and governance are distinct. They come from the same root, but they are not synonyms. Government is an institution. You can earn a university degree in government or political science; you can run for mayor or parliament or be hired as a county attorney, becoming part of the "ruling class." Government and political life are entwined. Many people regard human government as the cure-all for societies' problems, almost as a savior. Others see government as an evil; some see it as a necessary evil to tolerate, others as a scourge to cast off. But the notion of human government was God's idea. Government is an institution ordained by God.

Governance, on the other hand, is a discipline, a behavior, a way of life. Governance denotes order and management. An orderly life, for example, indicates healthy self-governance. Recall Abraham. He brought truth and the creation order to society. In this way he introduced self-governance. Self-governance, for the development of virtues in private as well as in the public square, remains essential for healthy societies. Os Guinness, tracing the discussion among the founders of the United States about the balance of freedom and virtue, points out that "leadership without character, business without ethics and science without human values—in short, freedom without virtue—will bring the republic to its knees."[10] The governance of a free republic had to rest on the self-governance of free citizens, for only those who can govern themselves as individuals can govern themselves as a people.[11]

Good internal self-governance is a prerequisite for external governance. Dr. Elizabeth Youmans has said it well: "Simply stated, the Christian principle of self-government is God ruling internally from the heart of the individual. In order to have true liberty, man must be governed internally by the

Spirit of God rather than by external forces. Government is first individual, then extends to the home, church, and the community."[12] Good governance means care for the land. Dominion over the forests. Nurturing human health. Agriculture. Development of the arts. Growth in the sciences, including governing sound waves. When radio signals carry messages of truth, goodness, and beauty, someone is exercising governance over sound waves!

Another important dimension of governing sound waves is controlling our words. In a society of free speech, we think we should be able to say whatever we want. But we are responsible to govern our words. And governed words begin with governed thoughts. When we don't govern our thoughts, our words are also ungoverned, and ungoverned words bring harm to us and to others. In a society of ungoverned words, external laws are written to enforce restraints that should be self-administered. Invariably, external laws multiply and freedom is diminished. But as Paul wrote to the Corinthians, "If we would judge ourselves, we would not be judged" (1 Cor. 11:31 NKJV).

Reflect

Describe the poverty/brokenness you see in the following:
- creation *- abused resources & earth*
- your nation *- deaths of unborn, deterioration of family units*
- your community *- divisive*
- your friends' lives *- God is not a focus or priority*
- your own life *- thoughts / words*

What is causing this brokenness?

THE DIFFERENCE BETWEEN WISDOM AND INTELLIGENCE

As we begin a book about wisdom, it's important to make a distinction. Intelligence is not the same thing as wisdom. When we speak of wisdom, we aren't talking about being smart. We have all met people who are smart but not wise. If you study long enough and hard enough, you can earn a PhD. You can be an expert in your field and be sought after for your knowledge. But many PhDs have little wisdom. By the same token, many people who have little formal education (knowledge) are nevertheless wise.

Wisdom is practicing behaviors that make life work; folly is repeating behaviors that result in brokenness. Wisdom leads to whole-life prosperity, to flourishing. Folly leads to whole-life poverty, to withering.

An educated fool makes terrible decisions. Many American politicians, for example, are regarded as brilliant. They are graduates from the best schools, such as Harvard and Yale. But often they lack wisdom. Intelligence is a gift from the Creator, but it is no substitute for wisdom. Wise decisions lead to flourishing. But many smart people live in folly, repeating behaviors that undermine human development. As Albert Einstein said, to do the same thing over and over and expect different results is the definition of insanity.

Walter Chalmers Smith (1824–1908) wrote a poem, later put to music, that captures this truth. The hymn, "Immortal, Invisible, God Only Wise," includes this stanza:

> To all life thou givest—to both great and small;
> In all life thou livest, the true life of all;
> We *blossom* and *flourish* as leaves on the tree,
> And *wither* and *perish*—but naught changeth thee.

God does not change. He is the one who gives us life. We, on the other hand, either "blossom and flourish" or "wither and perish." If we want to find the path of life, we must live in the framework God has made. To deny that framework, or to rebel against it, is to invite death.

Reflect

What does it mean for something to flourish? Health / growth

What causes something to flourish? Well attended to

What does it mean for something to wither? Unhealthy

What causes something to wither? Lack of care

Draw a picture that reflects flourishing and withering.

Identify conditions in your own life in which you have flourished. Debriefing - marriage in some areas

Identify conditions in your own life in which you have withered. Relationship w/ Seb

THE INTENDED AUDIENCE

This book is not for everyone. At the risk of losing the casual reader on the one hand and the academic on the other, we have written especially for thoughtful, activist practitioners with a global interest. We want to be of most impact where we believe we can be of most help.

Having said that, we are also writing for a larger readership, based on the common-ground character of Proverbs. Most people in the world wonder why their life isn't going well and want something better. People of all belief systems need to see the connection between wisdom and solving issues of poverty. We have worked to make the book accessible to people with little or no interest in the Bible. At the same time, Bible readers, especially those working with the poor or those trapped in cycles of poverty themselves, will be interested in the subject.

PREVIEW OF THE BOOK

A few words about the structure of the book will be helpful. In part 1 we deal with wisdom and the universe. How was wisdom involved in the creation? We talk about the *breadth* of wisdom as seen in the history of mankind. What link do we see between the cosmic reversal and wisdom, or the absence of wisdom? How does wisdom play into the sustaining of the universe? We will see that wisdom sustains the universe through divine providence (God's work) and through human obedience (our work). In the last section of part 1 we will look at the idea of wisdom and the consummation of the universe, a grand gathering up of human history into what J. R. R. Tolkien called a *eucatastrophe*, a good catastrophe.[13]

Part 2 will deal with the preeminence of wisdom. This will include reflections on Proverbs as a guidebook for life, a sort of manual to guide humans into a flourishing life.

In this part we treat three related words that appear all through Proverbs: knowledge, understanding, and wisdom. They are not synonymous. They are different, and wisdom is the highest of the three. Part 2 will end with a chapter we have titled "Worldly Wisdom versus Godly Wisdom." The term *wisdom* may be variously defined; we want to be clear that we are talking about wisdom as an attribute of God, and its application as a godly virtue in humans.

Part 3 is called "A World of Choices." We see two paths: the call of Lady Wisdom and the call of the prostitute. Throughout the book of Proverbs we are faced with twin choices. Will we listen to Wisdom or to the prostitute? We will see that we need to live with the end in mind. Most people live for the moment: a trip to the mall, a day at work, a weekend. Many cultures encourage instant gratification: unbridled sex, undisciplined eating, addictions of all kinds, unrestrained violent outbursts. We must see the end and live in light of that end. How will we choose between wisdom and folly, virtue and vice, prudence and naivete, and truthfulness and lying? This section will close with some models of flourishing.

All of this builds to the final part, "Wisdom and Development." Here we consider development in its multiple facets: moral, social, political, and economic. The book closes with a word about what price might be required for those who would follow the path of wisdom.

Throughout the book you will see opportunities to engage at a level deeper than just reading the narrative. We have developed three kinds of questions to help process the material and apply it more effectively: Prepare, Read, and Reflect.

At or near the beginning of most chapters (or sometimes the beginning of a section within a chapter) you will see a box labeled "Prepare" with suggested Scripture readings and questions to answer before beginning the chapter.

Within the chapters are boxes labeled "Read." You will find scriptures to be read and reflected on. These questions are meant to be answered in the context of the narrative at that point.

The third kind of study box, usually at the end of a chapter or section, is labeled "Reflect." These questions are designed to help you process what you have just read.

We encourage you to use these recommended exercises. They will significantly enrich your learning.

Part 1

Wisdom and the Universe

1

Wisdom Creates the Universe

Prepare

Read Genesis 1:1-5; John 1:1-3, 14; Hebrews 11:1-3.

How did God create?

What are the parallels between Genesis 1 and John 1?

What does faith allow us to understand?

Who am I? Why am I here? What does my life mean? Where is my life going? By the time we're eighteen years old we all ask those basic questions. Why does everyone wonder about such questions? That every human asks such questions suggests that the answers exist. Just as hunger suggests there is such a thing as food,[14] so questions about transcendence suggest there is such thing as metaphysical truth. And if there are answers, there must be an Answerer. One who has spoken. The Bible explains the meaning of human existence, the direction of history, and the nature of the world around us. The Bible gives meaning to life.

All of reality may be considered from two dimensions: breadth and depth. Let's say the breadth of reality is represented by the history of the world, the grand sweep of story from creation to today and beyond today to the end of time. By definition, the future is unknown to humans. But the Creator, the First Cause, is not constrained by human limitations. And about that future He has something to say. We'll come back to that.

Figure 1

If the *breadth* of reality is *history*, the *depth* of reality is the grand story of *meaning*, the sum of what is true, good, and beautiful (see fig. 1). These three—truth, goodness, and beauty—capture all that humans were created for. Sometimes this is referred to as the *cultural trinity*. To the extent that an individual is operating rationally, this cultural trinity captures all that he or she is seeking. To understand this fact is to be on the path of wisdom.

Read

Read Psalm 104:24; Proverbs 3:19; Jeremiah 10:12; 51:15.

What did God use to create the universe?

Read Proverbs 8:22–31.

When was wisdom "appointed to her task"?

How is wisdom described in the creation process?

Read Proverbs 3:19–20.

What three words are used to describe the work of creation?

What actions are associated with each word?

What might this signify?

Acting in His infinite wisdom, God created the universe. To emphasize the role of wisdom in the creation of the universe, the writer of Proverbs personified it. In Proverbs 8:27–31 wisdom testifies,

> When he established the heavens, I was there;
>> when he drew a circle on the face of the deep,
> when he made firm the skies above,
>> when he established the fountains of the deep,
> when he assigned to the sea its limit,
>> so that the waters might not transgress his command,
> when he marked out the foundations of the earth,
>> then I was beside him, like a master workman,
> and I was daily his delight,
>> rejoicing before him always,
> rejoicing in his inhabited world
>> and delighting in the children of man.

At the cosmic reversal, the universe fell into disarray, but wisdom remained. In fact, wisdom has sustained the universe ever since. The creation was broken, but wisdom holds it together. Someday, wisdom will lead to the consummation of the universe. But we're getting ahead of ourselves. Let's drill deeper into the creation story to see what it says about the role of wisdom in creation.

First of all, we see Trinitarian engagement in the creation. The Father speaks the words at creation, the Son carries out the decrees, the Holy Spirit moves over the face of the water. The Father is the speaker, the Son is the speech, the Holy Spirit is the speaking (the breath that carries the speech).

Acting in wisdom, God ordered creation with purposeful intention. One result: the human has unique significance. We see this in the way Genesis presents the stages of creation. God moved from less complex to more complex. First, He created time, space, and matter: "In the beginning [time], God created the heavens [space] and the earth [matter]" (Gen. 1:1). This summary statement is packed with meaning, which we will not develop here.[15] We simply note that all that happened in the creation is contained in this simple yet profound declaration. From there the record goes on to note the formation of inanimate creation: light, the heavens, water, the earth (1:2–10,

14–19). As the process continues, God makes plant life (1:11–13, 29–30) followed by animal life (that which has breath, 1:20–25).

All this is in preparation for the culmination of the created order, that which is made in the image of God Himself.

> Then God said, "Let us make man in our image, after our likeness. And let them have dominion over the fish of the sea and over the birds of the heavens and over the livestock and over all the earth and over every creeping thing that creeps on the earth." So God created man in his own image, in the image of God he created him; male and female he created them. And God blessed them. And God said to them, "Be fruitful and multiply and fill the earth and subdue it, and have dominion over the fish of the sea and over the birds of the heavens and over every living thing that moves on the earth." (Gen. 1:26–28)

Throughout the process, the writer records God's verdict of His creative work. Four times the writer adds "It was so" (Gen. 1:7, 9, 11, 15). Six times God pronounces "It [is] good" (1:4, 10, 12, 18, 21, 25) followed by the seventh with the superlative added, "It [is] very good" (1:31). No doubt you have completed a task—planting a garden, building a chair, clearing a field, painting a room, composing a song—and looked back with a sense of satisfaction. That satisfaction is a tiny echo of God's joy at the completion of His creation.

THE LORD OF HISTORY IS PURPOSEFUL

Philosophers and theologians use the term *ontology* to speak of the created purpose of all things. God is purposeful, never random or arbitrary in His intentions or actions. Another term that touches on this aspect of God's character in creation is *teleology*, that is, the end purpose to which all of history is moving. God created for a purpose and all of history is moving toward that final purpose. That leads to two important accompanying truths, one related to human existence and one to human activity.

First, contrary to the Darwinian premise, we do not exist by accident. The universe has a purpose. Your life has a purpose. All humans exist by God's purpose and intention, and your life as an individual has a purpose.

God knows you and created you for a purpose. Many young people wonder, *What's the purpose of my life? Everything is messed up. Nothing makes sense.* We all have these questions. But we are in a state of confusion about the answers because we have abandoned the creation order. At the fall, humans rejected wisdom. If we are to find clarity about the meaning of life, we must recover that wisdom.

The other truth that flows from God's purposeful nature is this: humans have responsibility to pursue God's intended purpose within the creation order. Just as increased order characterized God's creative work, human beings are to continue that progression. We are to take what God has given and dream dreams. We are to exercise our imaginations (another divine gift) and bring those inspirations into reality through our words and actions. This is inherent in Genesis 2:15, "The LORD God took the man and put him in the garden of Eden to work it and keep it."

Read

Read Genesis 1:29–30; Psalm 104:14–15.

What do you see when you see a seed?

Do you see the seed, or do you see the potential of the seed?

What does this suggest about the extent of your vision?

THE POWER OF THE SEED

We have all around us a powerful example of God's purposefulness in the creation. Consider an ordinary seed, whether from a tomato or apple, or the seeds at the top of tall grass or lying on the ground under a tree. Seeds were made to multiply. In this truth we have both a practical and symbolic reality. As human beings, descendants of the first couple fashioned by the Creator to tend the garden, we are responsible to find and use the purpose in each seed.

Too often we look at a seed and see no further than the husk. We fail to grasp what lies *inside* the seed, its amazing potential: the power to produce a plant, even a great tree that bears multiple fruits, each of which has multiple seeds. One seed can produce an entire orchard! One of my favorite African proverbs puts it like this: *You can count the seeds in a mango but you can't count the mangos in a seed!*

The essence of a seed is potential. A whole future lies locked inside every tiny seed. When God created the universe, He made it with virtually unlimited potential. That applies to all created life: plants, animals, humans. God made you with remarkable potential. Do you see that when you look in the mirror? It's true, whether you see it or not. In fact, most of us, most of the time, fail to see it. If we can imagine the forest in the seed, how much greater is the potential of your life?

We have examples of this "seed potential" everywhere. Recently I came across a wonderful story from Cateura, Paraguay, where a community of people are living off the proceeds of recycled items from a nearby landfill. A music teacher in the community had the vision to build a "recycled orchestra," instruments made from materials found in the dump.[16] In a place where a violin costs more than a house, young people are discovering the joy of music because someone had the vision to see the power of some "seeds" in the garbage.

Yes, our world is messed up in many ways. But to draw the conclusion that life has no purpose is to allow hardships to lead to despair. On the other hand, to see the power of the seed, to see that God built into the creation His intention of human flourishing, to see God's purposefulness in the seed, is to hear and heed the Word of God.

When I was teaching about this in Puerto Rico, two students shared stories that illustrate this principle.[17] Erin told us that every year she and her grandmother plant a garden. "We do not go to the store to buy vegetables; we grow our own vegetables. When we are planting, we do not simply see seeds. We see vegetables. We see corn on the cob and fried okra. This is our food."

Tito told the following story:

One day when I was seventeen, I was at the mall cinema with my friends. When we got out of the mall, I saw two guys, about eighteen or nineteen. They were apparently in a "romantic" relationship, hugging and kissing in public. But you could see in their faces that they were hurting and empty. My heart broke for them. I cried. I knew they were not created for this broken lifestyle of pain and drugs.

I thought, *Where would I be if I had not met God?* Isaiah wrote, "Like sheep we have gone astray. Every one of us has turned to his own way, and the Lord has laid on him the iniquity of us all."

We're all here [in this class] because someone believed in us, preached to us, believed that we could be what God designed us to be. *Where would I be if someone had not seen the potential I had?* I could not get the image of those guys out of my mind. All the people passing by seemed to be in their own world, didn't care if these guys perished. I went home and prayed that God would set them free and reveal Himself to them. We need to have faith that God can change people.

Read

Read Psalm 139:13-18; Jeremiah 29:11; 42:12; Matthew 13:31-32.

How would you interpret the message of these passages?

What is the purpose for which you and creation have been made?

What does it mean to flourish?

What is the opposite of flourishing?

MADE TO FLOURISH

As we have seen, God created seeds with limitless potential. He created seeds to bring flourishing. And that divine intention of flourishing runs through all creation.

Let's consider several English words that are important to understand as we think about flourishing. The following are the definitions found in Webster's 1828, our dictionary of choice.[18]

- *Prosper*: "To grow or increase; to thrive; to make gain; as, to prosper in business. Our agriculture, commerce and manufactures now prosper."
- *Thrive*: "To prosper by industry, economy and good management of property; to increase in goods and estate. A farmer thrives by good husbandry. . . . To grow; to advance; to increase or advance in anything valuable."
- *Flourish*: "1. To thrive; to grow luxuriantly; to increase and enlarge, as a healthy growing plant. 2. To be prosperous; to increase in wealth or honor."

- *Fruitful*: "1. Very productive; producing fruit in abundance; as fruitful soil; a fruitful tree; a fruitful season. 3. Plenteous; abounding in anything."

Reflect

What stands out for you in the definition of these words?

Give examples of flourishing and languishing in your own life. In your society.

COMPREHENSIVE FLOURISHING

As someone has wryly observed, there's no such thing as being a little bit pregnant. The same is true of flourishing. By definition, flourishing is comprehensive in its effect. A ten-year-old video-game wizard who can't read is not flourishing. A man who has abandons his family is not flourishing; neither is his family. A businessman who treats his employees poorly is not flourishing, nor is his business. When a farmer neglects his field, neither the human nor the land flourishes. A person cut off from the love of God is not flourishing.

When speaking of flourishing, we must speak comprehensively. Reality is both material and transcendent. Of course, the material is most readily visible. We can see physical poverty or wealth. We often address physical poverty and fail to recognize relational poverty. We are overly impressed with material wealth and don't see the often accompanying spiritual poverty. Moral and spiritual formation are foundational to all other dimensions of human flourishing. In fact, as our friend Elizabeth Youmans observes, the Hebrew word translated as "prosper" does not necessarily refer to material wealth, but means "to accomplish what is intended by God."[19]

Luke the physician once observed that the Messiah "increased in wisdom and in stature and in favor with God and man" (Luke 2:52). Several observations are worthy of note here. Note the growth in wisdom as well as physical, spiritual, and social dimensions. As a genuine human, Jesus grew physically from the moment of His conception through nine months of gestation. Following His birth, He experienced all the normal growth of childhood and youth. He grew in stature. He also grew in wisdom, the moral application of truth. In summary, the Messiah grew comprehensively, flourishing in every area of life. What a clear indication that God cares about all the dimensions of life! He went out of His way to see that this record was included in the Bible. The Messiah flourished comprehensively, and this becomes the model for our flourishing. We are to grow in wisdom, physically, in our relationship with God and with other humans.

Folly fails to recognize and acknowledge God. Wisdom sees God and His truth and brings His truth into our lives, like bringing beautiful music out of trash.

FRAMEWORK FOR FLOURISHING

Here's another important aspect of flourishing—again, a reflection of a creation principle. For something to flourish, it must function in accordance with its nature and design. Imagine a beautiful butterfly that couldn't fly. Or a whale unable to dive. If an orchard keeper finds a beautiful apple tree that doesn't bear fruit, he cuts it down!

In his wonderful book *The Evidential Power of Beauty*, Thomas Dubay elaborates on this. "Form is the deep root of a being's actuality, which gives it its basic whatness. It is the actualizing principle of a thing, the mysterious taproot that makes that thing to be what it is, and thus why it is different from every other kind of being. The inner form (not first of all an outer shape) of a palm tree makes it different from an oak, a corn stalk, indeed, a squirrel—even though all are made of atoms."[20] This is another way to say that any created thing flourishes according to its inherent nature and design. As Dubay says, "The splendor of a duck is limited to 'duckness' and that of an oak tree to 'oakness.'"[21]

Naturally, the principle extends to humanity. If a human being is to flourish, he or she must discover the design *with which* the Creator formed the human, and pursue the purpose *for which* the Creator made the human. We are not here as accidents of long eons of evolution. We are not merely animals or super-consumers. The human was made in the image of God. Our lives have meaning, our choices matter. Wisdom teaches us to function according to the Creator's purpose. Many people never learn this. As a result, their lives are marked by folly, never fulfilling their incredible God-given potential. In addition, their circle of friends and family miss the blessing of their flourishing. I know a gifted painter who, for some hidden reason, has not painted for twenty years. I think of how many people have missed the joy of seeing all the paintings this person has not painted, and the pleasure God has missed in seeing this person not fulfilling all the potential of their gifting.

WISDOM AND FOLLY

In the introduction we wrote about folly, the opposite of wisdom. Let's return now to consider some of the consequences of choosing folly rather than wisdom.

One way to begin reflecting about wisdom versus folly is by considering simple economics: How do wisdom and folly play out in the world of money? We find that by wisdom, wealth may be created and used to bless families and societies. But when we see wealth destroyed or stolen, we are seeing the fruits of folly.

Wisdom allows individuals and nations to create wealth.[22] Nations where a measure of wisdom has taken root have succeeded in building wealth and have provided for their people to rise above poverty.

Folly, on the other hand, influences individuals and nations to misuse wealth. Sometimes this presents as stealing. Others waste wealth with prodigal living. Some destroy wealth by irresponsible behavior or even anarchy. Some destroy wealth through corrupt practices, including government policies that destroy initiative. I recently visited Cuba. Cuba is a paradise, with incredible agricultural potential and an imaginative and innovative people. But government policies have stifled the potential of her citizens and impoverished her people. All these foolish behaviors have consequences. When we violate God's order by destroying wealth or crippling potential, we are causing others (and ourselves) to flounder rather than flourish.

But not all wealth, nor all poverty, is material. Both are comprehensive in nature. On a visit to New York City, Mother Teresa made an observation that no doubt surprised many people: "I've never seen such poverty as I've seen here." You could consider Mother Teresa something of an expert on poverty, so her assessment has meaning. Surrounded by the glitz and glamor and opulence of America's most famous city, she saw poverty. What did she mean? She was speaking about moral and spiritual poverty. Wisdom calls us and enables us to develop comprehensively, but comprehensive poverty ensues from folly.

People who work in the world of finance talk a lot about "capital." What is capital? Webster's 1828 dictionary offers the following definition: "the sum of money or stock which a merchant, banker or manufacturer employs in his business; either the original stock, or that stock augmented. Also, the sum of money or stock which each partner contributes to the joint fund or stock of the partnership; also, the common fund or stock of the company, whether incorporated or not."

Mostly, when people speak of capital, they are referring to material resources. But just as not all wealth or poverty is material, not all capital is material. There is a metaphysical capital inherent within every human being. Humans were created in the image of the Creator. They have the ability to develop new ideas, dream new dreams, imagine new worlds. Look around you. Whatever you see beyond the natural world has come from this God-given inner capital of a human. Every book ever written, every building ever constructed, every song ever composed, every technology ever invented, every sculpture ever formed, every garden ever cultivated—all of these came to fruition because of the metaphysical capital of the human mind.

Wisdom calls us to steward this internal capital, as well as the external capital of creation, to mimic God's creative activity by producing culture that glorifies God.

Encyclopedia: The Circle of Knowledge

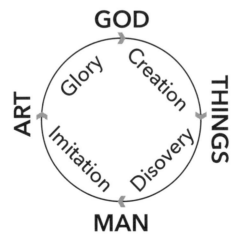

Figure 2

One way to picture this is the Circle of Knowledge (see fig. 2).[23] Beginning at the top we see that God is the primary Creator. God's *ex nihilo* (out-of-nothing) work resulted in the primary creation (things). God created the universe with mysteries built into it. He did this with the intention that man would explore the creation and discover the mysteries. "It is the glory of God to conceal things, but the glory of kings is to search things out" (Prov. 25:2).

Man, made in the image of God, is the secondary creator. Man discovers truth that God has placed in the creation. Man discovers through three "books": "the book of revelation known through the Scriptures, the book of nature known inductively through the senses, and the book of the mind—which was logic."[24] Man discovers and then imitates the Creator. God creates out of nothing; man creates from raw materials in the primary creation and produces art, technology, systems, and ideas. Man creates to the glory of God. He manifests the Primary Creator and the primary creation through his creative activity.

Earlier we wrote about the Landfill Harmonic. Children in the garbage dump discovered beauty! They transformed "garbage" into musical instruments and inspiring music. This is an example of the secondary creation.

When we create art and culture, we are imitating God. We are to create art and culture that honors the Primary Creator and reflects His primary creation. When we do, we bring glory to God and joy to our fellow human beings. At the end of history, this will culminate in the earth being filled with the knowledge of God. None of this could happen in a world of spontaneous generation. Too many people know that intellectually but fail to live it in life and wisdom.

MODELS OF FLOURISHING

Earlier we referenced the multiple dimensions in the growth of the Messiah: growth in wisdom as well as in the physical, social, and spiritual dimensions.

Jun Vencer is chairman of the board of trustees of the Alliance Graduate School in the Philippines. Dr. Vencer is one of the world's leading thinkers on wholistic development. He has encapsulated the concept of flourishing on a national level as follows:

- individual and national righteousness
- economic sufficiency for all

- lasting social peace
- lasting public justice, even for the poorest of the poor[25]

THE ORDER OF CREATION

The opposite of order is disorder. God built order into the creation. Human flourishing comes from following the order built into the creation. By the same token, abandoning order—pursuing disorder—results in human withering. God's creation order affirms the sacredness of human life, the sacredness of one-man and one-woman marriage, the dignity of work. When these creation principles are twisted or abandoned, disorder and poverty follow.

In a class discussion on this topic, a young woman named Nilka shared the following story.

> In Puerto Rico we have a generation that does no work or study. We call them *nini*. They are in their early twenties and have the capacity to work but don't feel guilty about being dependent on others. Their attitude is, *Work is bad. Why work?* If they can be dependent on their parents or grandparents, they are happy to do that.
>
> One of these young men wanted to hang out with me. I was co-leader of a youth group and had duties. I told him, "I have responsibilities, so if you want to help me, you can hang out and help." He agreed. In the process he met some of the young men in our group. He discovered people who were not like his own friends, whose behaviors were discouraging. The fellows in the youth group treated him well, respected him, did not encourage him to do bad things. He was seeing the difference between the culture of the group and that of his friends.
>
> Sometimes we went to the university library. He would sit and do nothing but watch me read. "What are you doing?" he would ask me. "What are you reading?" So I started reading aloud to help him learn. He began to expand his knowledge of things in a way he had never before because he had never studied. We were studying neurons of the brain. I explained to him what a neuron is as I would explain it to a child. That way I was learning and he was learning at the same time.

Little by little he learned about God, as well as politics, science, and psychology. This happened over a semester. Now he has registered in a junior college and is studying refrigeration. He is excited and is at the top of his class.

Of course, the type of people whom Puerto Ricans call *nini* live in lots of places. In August 2013, Fox News broadcast a special report titled "The Great Food Stamp Binge." Fox conducted a poll indicating that 74 percent believed that "Americans rely too much on the government and not enough on themselves." The ultimate example was a twenty-nine-year-old man named Jason Greenslate. In the broadcast Greenslate told the interviewer about his life as a California beach bum happily living on welfare, partying, and eating lobster bought with government-issued food stamps. "Why not?" he asked.

Greenslate's question effectively captures the issue. If the universe is the product of chance played out over innumerable years of evolution, if there is no Creator who fashioned and sustains the world around us, if there is no metaphysical reality . . . why should anyone attempt to live according to any order?

The evidence suggests otherwise.

2

Wisdom Sustains the Universe

The late Dr. Howard Hendricks of Dallas Theological Seminary was well known as a highly effective professor. One of his topics related to the importance of listening when we find ourselves in the presence of greatness. Hendricks told the story of sitting on an airplane next to the famous actor Charlton Heston, who portrayed Moses in the 1956 Cecil B. DeMille movie *The Ten Commandments*. For Hendricks it was an opportunity to ask questions, listen, and learn. But some people would miss the moment by trying to impress a man of Heston's stature, rather than listen. Like the youth who reads a book on business and tries to lecture his father, a successful business owner, on markets and profits. Or the teenage guitarist showing off to a professional musician. Or the novice cook who corners a master chef at a party to detail how she fricassees chicken.

We should recognize the value in those who have achieved renown over a lifetime of discipline and sustained performance. They have much to impart, and we can learn from them. Those who are wise know how to listen to people like this.

If that's true, how much more important and valuable to heed the instruction of the God who created the universe. He who commanded it into existence is the same God that preserves, governs, and guides that creation. He created it in wisdom; He sustains it in wisdom. In this chapter and the next, we will consider three parts of this truth. First, wisdom sustains the universe through three converging streams: creation laws, God's divine providence, and human obedience. If we would flourish, if we want to achieve all that God intends for us, we need a clear grasp of these three aspects of wisdom.

WISDOM SUSTAINS THE UNIVERSE THROUGH CREATION LAWS

God governs the universe through laws and ordinances. We use the term *creation laws* to describe these laws, which broadly fit into three categories: truth (physical and metaphysical laws), beauty (aesthetic laws), and goodness (moral laws).

Truth, another term for reality, encompasses both the physical and the metaphysical realm, the way the universe really exists, external to us and our worldview (the way we see the world).

The physical laws that help define the physical universe aren't laws in the sense of commands, such as "Thou shalt not steal" or even "Stop." In this case "law" references a physical law, a law of nature. Webster's 1828 dictionary defines law as "the determination of a body to certain motions, changes, and relations, which uniformly take place in the same circumstances."[26] Among these are the law of motion discovered by Johannes Kepler, the law of gravity discovered by Isaac Newton, and the laws of thermodynamics. All these laws are necessary for sustaining human life on earth.

Metaphysical laws are the "internal framework." For example, Thomas Cahill writes about the "Temple of the Spirit, an inner landscape of ideas and feelings."[27] Our worldview, our mental infrastructure, entails metaphysical laws.[28] These include our understanding of the nature of the transcendent universe (it is relational), the nature of man (we are made in the image of God), and the creation itself (it is more than material, it is an open system).[29]

Beauty circumscribes the aesthetic order. Beauty is a law, an objective standard, just as truth is an objective standard. Does that sound unlikely? Many people, even those who believe in absolute truth, are relativists when it comes to beauty. It's fashionable to declare, "beauty is in the eye of the beholder." I have said that in the past, until I was challenged by Thomas Dubay's book, mentioned previously, *The Evidential Power of Beauty*. Dubay argues that beauty comes from God. Of all that is beautiful, God is most beautiful. Thus, God's nature of beauty establishes the criterion for beauty. Beauty is not in the eyes of the beholder. Yes, we all have our favorite colors; some people prefer red over blue. But that does not mean that beauty itself is a wholly subjective matter. This is a concept of modern relativism. Beauty is in the glory of God.

Finally, we come to the word that captures the moral order: goodness. Relativism has shredded much of the notion of goodness. Forty years ago theologian Francis Schaeffer pointed out that to tell a modern young woman to "be a good girl" was increasingly to speak nonsense. The loss of an objective moral code in the West has wrought unspeakable grief and harm. In contrast, the Ten Commandments represent the moral order of the universe. These are not arbitrary moral codes on the order of "no shirt, no shoes, no service." These are laws. To keep them is to walk on the path to thriving; to abandon them leads to death. God made the universe to function by laws. He governs the universe through creation laws.

Truth, beauty, goodness—all three derive from God. All that is true reflects God, who created the universe in truth, who dwells in the realm of truth, who invented everything that is true. All that is false opposes God and His nature. In the same way, all that is beautiful, all that is good, echoes the ultimate beauty and goodness that is God Himself.

Wisdom and God's laws are inseparably linked.

Read

Read Deuteronomy 4:5-6; Deuteronomy 29:9; Psalm 19:7-10.

What do these verses reveal about wisdom and God's laws?

CREATION'S LAWS

At the back of my (Gary's) yard a fence divides my property from my neighbor's property. Some people argue that fences and boundaries are bad. They are too harsh, too selfish. But clear boundaries help establish peaceful relationships. In ranching country where it's important to keep cattle separate, I have heard the sentiment, "Good fences make good neighbors." Without fences cattle would mingle, and confusion about who owns which cows would quickly ensue. The fence between me and my neighbor establishes a very helpful boundary.

In the same way, we live in a universe with boundaries. Creation's laws establish the divide between truth and falsehood, between good and evil, between beauty and deformity. They reveal the direction a person or nation is moving: toward life or death, flourishing or perishing.

The universe has boundaries. We may not like the boundaries, but they are real. And, as even a brief reflection will make clear, they are helpful. Important. Necessary, even.

Read

Read Psalm 33:11; Isaiah 14:24; Malachi 3:6; Hebrews 13:8; James 1:17.

What do these passages reveal about the following?
- the nature of God
- the nature of God's laws and ordinances

GOD'S LAWS ARE IMMUTABLE

The Bible teaches the immutability of God: God does not change. "God is unchanging in the perfection of His nature, character, purposes (will), and promises."[30] God's laws are also immutable.

> Of old you laid the foundation of the earth,
>   and the heavens are the work of your hands.
> They will perish, but you will remain;
>   they will all wear out like a garment.
> You will change them like a robe,
>   and they will pass away,
> but you are the same,
>   and your years have no end. (Ps. 102:25–27)

The uniformity of the laws of nature is a constant revelation of the immutability of God. What they were at the beginning of time they are still today. They apply in every part of the universe. No less stable are the laws which regulate the operation of reason and conscience. The whole governance of God, as the God of nature and as moral governor, rests on the immutability of His counsels.

Earlier we pointed to gravity as an example of a creation law. Gravity is unavoidable. It's always in effect. The fact is, all God's laws are both immutable (unchanging) and inviolable (unbreakable). This is part of the design of the universe, a reflection of God's purposes. Thomas Dubay writes that the creation is "stunningly specific." The universe was designed and purposed for the existence of human beings. Dubay quotes R. P. McCabe: "The conditions at zero time plus one milli-second were what they were precisely because they lead to human life. There is, scientifically speaking, an imperative connection between the first seconds of the observable physical universe and man."[31] Dubay continues, "The universe requires incredibly complex mathematical formulas to explain how it is and how it operates. Which, of course, means that it demands a supreme Mind to make it to be what it is. No book of algebra or geometry or trigonometry comes to be by random change."[32]

The universe was formed according to God's purposes. Human beings are to live within this form to flourish. We are subject to real laws and ordinances—the decrees of God's creation order that govern our lives.

Freedom is found when we recognize this truth and live within this design, the place we are most alive. On the other hand, to ignore or reject this truth, to refuse to live within this design, results in enslavement. In the water, a salmon is perfectly free. It has the ideal environment for finding food and thriving. A salmon that decided to abandon that environment, to live on a grassy riverbank, would not be free. Nor would it survive. A pelican freely flying over coastal waters in the company of its fellows seeking a mouthful of anchovies is the picture of a creature living in the freedom of God's design. If such a bird could decide, *I want to swim in the sea*, it would very quickly lose all freedom. A fish is made to swim, a bird to fly.[33]

In the world of technology, the same is true. The Boeing Company makes vehicles for flight, not for running on parallel steel tracks. That's the domain of locomotives.

Read

Read Deuteronomy 11:8-9; Proverbs 4:20-22; 8:35-36.

Describe the relationship between living within the framework of God's laws and experiencing life and well-being.

Describe the relationship between revolting against God's laws and experiencing sickness and death.

LIFE AND DEATH

In 1911 Robert Sadler was born into a sharecropping family in South Carolina. When he was five, Robert was sold into slavery. He tells the gut-wrenching story in his book *The Emancipation of Robert Sadler: The Powerful True Story of a Twentieth-Century Plantation Slave.*[34]

> "Git over there by the house and stand still!" [Father] ordered us roughly. We did as we were told and when we turned around, Father was in the wagon and spiraling it back the way we had come. I called out to him, but he didn't turn his head. Then Pearl called, "Father, wait! Don't leave us!" and she ran after the wagon. It was no use. Father didn't even look at her. His fierce gaze was on the road ahead of him, and he didn't pay any mind to our cries and pleas.
>
> The wagon disappeared down the driveway and onto the main road. Pearl and Margie and I stood trembling against the side of the house, our feet digging into the cold earth. It was spring of 1917 and my sisters and I had just been sold as slaves.

Robert courageously escaped slavery in 1925, sixty-two years after the Emancipation Proclamation. Yet many people in his community continued to suffer as slaves. A nation can make slavery illegal, but that does not remove a slave mentality from all its citizens.

I (Darrow) saw another illustration of this principle in Brazil recently. My host took me past a landfill to show me some apartments the government had built for people living on the dump. They furnished the apartments with electricity, running water, and flush toilets. They moved everyone off the dump into these apartments. Six months later the people were living on the garbage dump again. Someone in the government had a compassionate idea to create apartments for these people. But they did not take into account the "garbage dump" in the peoples' minds. Taking the people out of the dump was hard; getting the dump out of the people is even harder. Changing the way we think about ourselves, about what we have always considered "normal," requires a change in our worldview.

When we choose to live outside the framework of creation laws, we experience horrible consequences: alienation, ugliness, destruction, and death.

By the same token, living within that framework generally results in a more abundant life. E. Stanley Jones, in his book *The Unshakable Kingdom and the Unchanging Person*, writes of the observation of a Swedish surgeon, "I've discovered the kingdom of God at the end of my scalpel—it is in the tissues. The right thing morally, the Christian thing, is always the healthy thing physically."[35] The surgeon sees reality, the kingdom of God, evidence of God's creation, in the human body. He does not see mere tissue, but God-ordained life.

Read

Read Psalm 19:7–14.

How does the psalmist David describe the commands of the Lord?

Make a list of how he describes
- their nature
- their benefits

Who enjoys the benefit of following Gods laws? Is it only Jews and Christians? Why or why not?

THE NATURE OF THE UNIVERSE

I (Gary) met a man on a plane who told me that none of what we could see was real. All of this—the plane, the people, the clouds visible outside the window—was simply an illusion. I reminded him that he had gone to a lot of bother (booking the trip, buying the ticket, arranging his schedule, driving to the airport, etc.) for an illusion, but he was not deterred.

Look around you. Contrary to the teachings of Hinduism, the universe is real! It is not *maya*, an illusion, as Hinduism teaches.[36] Nor is the universe merely material, as the secularist would say, trying to deny the moral and spiritual realms.

And, what is more, the universe is good. The Creator so declares it. In contrast to Eastern faiths that see the world as something to flee, the Bible assigns value to the creation even after the fall. Its Maker affirms that it is good.

> The earth is the LORD's and the fullness thereof,
>   the world and those who dwell therein,

for he has founded it upon the seas
>   and established it upon the rivers. (Ps. 24:1–2)

The creation is a comprehensive and integrative whole, material and spiritual. It is marked by order and not chaos. The Creator expects the material world—individuals, communities, and nations—to flourish, to make progress, not to be static. Nor are humans to be impoverished. They are to flourish.

Earlier we talked about the universal need for boundaries. We mentioned that the creation laws function as boundaries. Let's return to that concept for some further elaboration. Boundaries may be physical, moral, metaphysical, or aesthetic. Gravity is an example of a physical boundary. It's easy to see it in action, every day, all day. A baby in a high chair discovers, with great delight, the law of gravity—dropping food on the floor to watch it recede in the distance. That same baby learning to walk, or the child learning to ride a bicycle, will find the gravity boundary less delightful.

The creation also includes moral boundaries. We find this in the Decalogue, otherwise known as the Ten Commandments. In these ten laws, the Creator drew a circle around human behaviors that lead to flourishing, behaviors that bless others and bring joy to oneself. When we violate this moral boundary—by committing adultery, for example—we bring grief and injury to ourselves, our spouse, our children, and others. Just as we can be physically injured by ignoring the law of gravity, we will be personally (and often permanently) injured when we ignore moral boundaries.

A third category of creation boundary is the metaphysical, that is, those aspects of truth that deal with the nature of God, man, and creation. What is God like? What is the purpose of the human? How do the various parts and dimensions of the universe work together? When we answer these questions, we are dealing in metaphysical boundaries. For example, when we embrace the idea that man is an animal, a product of spontaneous generation gradually evolving from simple life-forms over eons of time, we are moving outside the creation metaphysical boundary which establishes man as a creature made in God's image. When we reduce God to something less than the infinite, eternal Creator, we have stepped outside the metaphysical boundaries that govern life and we suffer as a result.

Finally, the creation includes aesthetic boundaries, as we discussed earlier around the idea of an objective standard of beauty based on the nature of God Himself.

> **Prepare**
>
> Read Psalm 19:1-4; Proverbs 25:2; Romans 1:19-20.
>
> What does creation do?
>
> What is mankind's role?

CREATION COMMUNICATES

All that we have discussed so far implies a fundamental principle to which we will now turn: God is not silent. He has spoken. He has revealed Himself. The term *revelation* carries the sense of that which we cannot know unless God chooses to tell us. But He has told us. God has revealed things to us. He shows us His existence and His nature through the "books" of revelation: the book theologians call *special* revelation—the Bible, and the book that is common to all human beings—the creation. The latter includes the book of nature and the book of reason. Truth is found at the intersection of these three books: the Bible, nature, and reason, with the Bible the ultimate authority of the three. Figure 3 depicts an early seal of Harvard University, which was meant to represent the three books of Scripture, nature, and reason.[37] Notice that one book is turned upside down; this is meant to depict the limits of human reason and the need for God's revelation.[38]

Figure 3

Creation reveals God's existence and His nature; these are "understood through what has been made" (Rom. 1:20). Creation reveals God to all who will observe that creation through two avenues: the senses (in other words, through science, as argued by Aristotle) and reason (as argued by Plato). If we believe that the natural world—the universe—is the work of a Creator, it follows that His creation tells us something about Him. Let's look more closely at the book of science (nature) and the book of reason.

Science witnesses that God has made the universe wisely; it is orderly, it yields to His ordinances, and it is intelligible. Man has been made in the image and likeness of God and thus can explore the universe that God has made. Man can discover its hidden secrets and uncover its codes. As the psalmist has said, *the universe communicates*:

> The heavens declare the glory of God;
>> the skies proclaim the work of his hands.
> Day after day they pour forth speech;
>> night after night they display knowledge.
> There is no speech or language
>> where their voice is not heard.
> Their voice goes out into all the earth,
>> their words to the ends of the world. (Ps. 19:1–4)

God's creation declares His glory, day after day, night after night, through all generations to the ends of the earth. The creation is a constant source of revelation about God's existence and glory.

Similarly, the apostle Paul wrote to the Romans: "For the wrath of God is revealed from heaven against all ungodliness and unrighteousness of men, who by their unrighteousness suppress the truth. For what can be known about God is plain to them, because God has shown it to them. For his invisible attributes, namely, his eternal power and divine nature, have been clearly perceived, ever since the creation of the world, in the things that have been made. So they are without excuse" (Rom. 1:18–20).

Let's look at the knowledge revealed here:

- God has revealed Himself to all who will see.
- He has done so through His creation.

- He has revealed
    - o the reality of His existence;
    - o something of His invisible attributes, that is, His eternal power and divine nature.
- These things are not hidden but are *clearly* seen.
- They have been revealed to all peoples, through all times, since the beginning of the world.
- These things are so clear so that no human being has an excuse to be ignorant of God. No one can say, "I didn't know!"
- Those who deny God are *actively suppressing* the truth.

Because of this, God is to be sought after and recognized in all of creation—in the natural, the supernatural, and His miraculous intervention in history. Indeed, from the standpoint of the Bible, there is no such thing as an atheist. As we saw in the words of Paul, the truth is plain to them: God has made it plain to them but they have suppressed the truth. All people know that God exists, but they choose to suppress that knowledge, to push it down and away, out of their mind. This is folly and leads to brokenness and despair.

A third book of revelation is the book of the mind. Man, made in the image of God, possesses reason, creativity, emotions, and will. Man has the ability to discover the laws of nature and nature's God, the ability to "think God's thoughts after Him," as the German scientist Johann Kepler put it. Man's ability to reason, to use logic, is a gift from the Creator that He intends us to use.

Some fundamentalist faith systems deny the use of human reason. The human mind is seen as a liability to be avoided rather than a God-given asset to be used. But this approach cripples human growth and flourishing. Human beings are made in the image of God (*imago Dei*). They can look at their own existence, their creativity, their longings to love and be loved, and can conclude there is more to their lives than mere physical existence.

All three books of revelation—nature, the Bible, and reason—are necessary to guide human development. When these three books of revelation come together, the result is knowledge, understanding, and wisdom.

WISDOM SUSTAINS THE UNIVERSE THROUGH DIVINE PROVIDENCE

Here's a second principle about how wisdom sustains the universe: it does so through divine providence. God works providentially through His laws to sustain the universe.

Providence must do with God's preserving and governing of the universe. In wisdom, and through wisdom, God preserves (sustains) the creation. It may be helpful to think of this in two parts or principles: (1) God built order into the universe; He established creation ordinances; and (2) God rules through those ordinances.

> ### Read
>
> Read Colossians 1:15-17; Hebrews 1:2-3.
>
> What do these verses reveal about God's involvement with the universe?

GOD BUILT THE CREATION WITH ORDER

God built order into the universe. He established what is sometimes called *creation ordinances* or boundaries into the creation.

Before we explore creation ordinances, we need to make a related observation: God exists outside the creation. That will strike some readers as redundant, but many people do not operate with this essential understanding of the relationship between God and the universe. Theologians speak of the Creator-creature distinction. There is God, and there is everything else. Everything besides God was made by God. God transcends the creation. He is transcendent. He existed before the universe and continues to exist outside it.

And yet God is not remote. In fact, God is immanent as well as transcendent. He is very much present in the universe, and His presence includes activity, work, governance. God works in space and time; He providentially governs the creation. We can think of this as the worldview of the Bible.[39]

One scholar puts it like this: "We may define Divine Providence as Infinite Wisdom, using infinite power to accomplish the ends of infinite holiness and love."[40]

WORLDVIEW AND PROVIDENCE

Providence may be described, generally, as the relationship between God and His creatures, especially human beings, who are vice-regents of creation. Like everything else, one's view of that question is part of the larger picture of one's view of all reality. Which is another way to say one's worldview.

Is God actively involved in world affairs? Maybe He impassively watches the "game" of human history from on high. Or maybe there's no God at all. Or maybe what we think of as "God" is actually an impersonal force that runs under and through the world that we see, that gives life and unity to all living things but is not actually a person.

All of these are given as answers to the question of divine providence. And each is determined by the larger worldview one holds. One's worldview determines one's view of providence. Let's consider four common worldview possibilities and how they speak to this question of God and the universe.

Judeo-Christian worldview. Reality demonstrates that God is the creator and sustainer of the universe. He is both transcendent and immanent. God built laws into the universe. These are the creation ordinances. God actively governs through divine providence. This is seen generally—for example, His governing by established laws as well as actively (i.e., His breaking into time and space more directly).

Deism. The deist says God created the universe to run on laws and then walked away from the creation. In this view, God exists as creator but the universe is on autopilot. The universe is "self-governing" by means of the natural/physical laws. Providence only exists in a general, mechanical sense; God does not break into time and space.

Atheism. This view denies the existence of God. There is no God and thus no natural God-ordained law. The only reality is that which is physical and "natural." Since there is no God, there is no divine providence. Atheistic scientists must assume order to do their work, but they have no explanation for it and profess to deny it.

Animism (neo-paganism). A fourth system rises from an ancient religion that is now reemerging. Animism sees the universe as alive, a biological organism. This is sometimes called the "Gaia principle." There is no personal god, no divine providence. At best, there is a mysterious "impulse" to life. The movie *Avatar* is a propaganda piece for neo-paganism. Nature is alive. There's no natural law ordained by God.

GOD PROVIDENTIALLY RULES CREATION THROUGH CREATION ORDINANCES

In chapter 1 we saw that wisdom created the universe. Now we see that wisdom also sustains the universe. God providentially rules creation through His creation ordinances. God acts providentially to rule creation in two ways: He works *through* His established laws, and sometimes He *suspends* those laws. Normally, God works providentially to rule creation by acting through the creation ordinances. This is not the deistic concept of the universe on "auto-pilot" using natural laws. No, the Law Giver is actively engaged in governing through these laws.

The story of European colonizers of the New World powerfully illustrates this divine governance of creation laws. In their remarkable book, *The Puritan Gift: Reclaiming the American Dream Amidst Global Financial Chaos*, authors Ken Hopper and Will Hopper trace the story of how the Puritans, the third wave of British colonizers, learned from the failures of the first two groups.

The initial wave left England for Jamestown in December 1606. But neglecting to plan appropriately, they landed on the shores of Virginia in winter, their provisions depleted. Short on food and exposed to the elements, only 38 of the original 144 survived the first year. The Pilgrim wave of 1620 fared little better. They arrived in New England on November 10. They sailed the Atlantic during good weather, but arrived too late to plant crops and spent the winter trying to build houses, and lost half their company in the first three months.

In contrast to both, the Puritans, who began arriving in 1630, learned from these disasters and planned carefully and thoroughly. They sailed the Atlantic in inclement winter weather in order to arrive in time to plant their crops and build shelter before the next winter. They recruited people with skills necessary to successfully establish a colony and brought the kind and quantity of provisions required to survive and flourish.

As a result they succeeded where the earlier attempts at establishing colonies did not. The Puritans not only learned from history, they also understood the concept of governance and were gifted and thoughtful planners and managers. They took into account the times and season.[41] Instead of suffering privations, starvation, and death, they flourished and grew. As the Hoppers discovered, "the gift of the Puritans" was their management culture. They argue that it was this culture that caused the New World to prosper and flourish.

God rules the creation by means of the creation ordinances, but He also rules by supernaturally working around those ordinances.[42] There are times when, for His purposes, God may suspend the creation laws to break into space and time more directly. When this happens we witness what are called "miracles." God put a path through the Red Sea so the Hebrews could walk through and be free from slavery. He parted the Jordan River allowing His people to walk on dry ground into the promised land.

God alone made the universe; His *ex nihilo* creation bears witness to His unique and manifest glory. God alone rules providentially all the affairs of the creation. In wisdom, He sustains His beloved creation. We cannot flourish without understanding these truths and shaping our lives accordingly.

What is more, God has made a place for us in the sustaining and flourishing of His magnificent creation. To this truth we now turn.

Reflect

Draw a picture of what you have learned in this session.

What does it mean to live within the circle of reality?

3

Wisdom Sustains the Universe
through Human Obedience

Years ago I (Gary), with my wife, came home with a load of groceries. While we were putting everything away, I took a brick of cheese out of a bag and set it aside (in an inconspicuous spot) for a moment so I could quickly reach something that needed to go into the freezer. Then I forgot about the cheese. I didn't come across it for a couple of weeks. When I did, it was ruined. Of course! This is evidence of what science calls the second law of thermodynamics. One could put it in layman's terms, things deteriorate over time.[43] When you take a freshly baked angel food cake out of the oven, it's soft and delicious. But if you leave it on the counter for several days it will get hard and unappealing. On the other hand, a fresh cracker is crisp right out of the bag, but a few days' exposure will leave it soft and unappetizing! This creation law is always active.[44] Much of the time, for most of us, these laws are invisible. We can ignore them (and suffer the consequences) or try to deny them, but we can't change them. They are law.

In the last chapter we discussed the question of how wisdom sustains the universe. We suggested this happens in three ways. First, through God's creation laws. God governs through laws and ordinances. These laws and ordinances are part of what God in wisdom uses to sustain the creation. God is proactive in governing, and He uses laws and ordinances in that process.

A second way in which wisdom governs the universe is God's active breaking into time and space. God sometimes suspends His laws. We often call that a miracle. God breaks through ordinary history with out-of-the-ordinary action. Normally He allows His laws to rule without interruption. Sometimes He proactively suspends them.

SUSTAINED THROUGH HUMAN OBEDIENCE

Now let's consider the third way in which wisdom sustains the universe: through human obedience. God created. He made man and gave him the ability and the responsibility to act as a steward of the creation. A steward is one who manages the property of another. In the wisdom of God, He delegated a measure of creation care to man. Wisdom sustains the universe through human obedience.

God is sovereign and yet humans have a measure of freedom. We are made in the image of God. God has delegated authority to us.

This is not an ivory-tower theory; it's a cosmic truth with enormous implications. This is especially true because of the brokenness of the world—that is, the moral, natural, and institutional evils all around us. God has shared with humans the responsibility to address that brokenness. We are to be stewards of our own lives, of our relationships with others, and of the rest of creation. God wants each of us to flourish. He made us for a purpose and intends that purpose to be fulfilled in our lives. But when we act without wisdom, things get broken, as we saw earlier in the difference between wisdom and folly.

Reflect

List ways you see brokenness between the following:
- a human being and his/her God
- a human being and herself/himself (personal brokenness)
- human beings and creation

What examples of brokenness have you seen in your own society?

Today we see profound brokenness in many societies: the evil of sex slavery, other forms of slavery, the caste system, tribalism, and sexism. Think also of the consequences of natural evils such as drought, disease, and hunger. All of these are examples of brokenness that comes from human folly. What would wisdom say about each of these?

God governs through wisdom, and we help govern the universe through our obedience.

Stewarding the earth—another way to speak of sustaining the universe—is a shared responsibility. Divine providence does not work independently of man's free will. God rules and may overrule through His providence, but He does not destroy human freedom and responsibility. This carries many implications, including the following:

- Human work is a creation gift from God. He expects us to use our creativity to engage in the development of the creation.
- God, as Creator, can intervene in all aspects of the creation.
- If we govern like God, if we imitate Him, we will govern with wisdom.
- When we govern according to God's ordinances, good things naturally result.

Some of these we will develop in what follows.

Humankind was made to rule in God's stead. From the standpoint of privilege, humans are vice-regents, the kings and queens of God's creation. From the standpoint of responsibility, human beings are accountable, under the sovereign rule of their Creator, for the future of their own lives, the health and well-being of their families, the welfare of their communities, and the building of their nations.

THE GREAT *AND*

One of the saddest situations for a human being is to exist without meaningful relationships. Except for revered monks, nobody considers a hermit lifestyle to be exemplary. Nobody envies the elderly widow abandoned by her family in a care center. Our hearts go out to an orphan shuffled from one foster home to another. Why are these stories so sad? Because we are made for relationship. In fact, the universe is built on relationships. We see this at multiple levels.

The first relationship in the creation is the One and the Many of the Trinity, God in three persons. This foundational aspect of God's nature lies under every other relationship in the universe. In fact, because God is one God in three persons—because God is inherently relational—all other relationships exist. If we remove the foundation of this plurality (plurality, not multiplicity) of God, we lose the basis for all other relational aspects of the world. For example, the relational nature of God gives meaning to the relationship between God and His creation. He is not a distant, remote clockmaker who wound up the universe and walked away. God is immanent, actively indwelling His creation.

The relationship between God and His people also derives from this relational nature of God. He is Father. His people are His children. He loves with the love of a father. Indeed, every good father is a little picture of God's fathering nature.

Here's another example of relationship in the creation: that between the man and the woman. God formed the first man from the dust of the ground. From the man's rib He formed the woman. The very terms in the Hebrew picture the depth of the relationship inherent in this creation method. "She shall be called *Isha*, woman, because she was taken from *Ish*, man" (Gen. 2:23). One flesh was divided into Ish and Isha. Then, in a creative act as poetic as it is profound, God brings Ish and Isha together to make one flesh. Thus we have in the two-in-one human a derivative reflection of the Three-in-One God.

Finally, there is the link between humankind and creation. As *imago Dei* creatures, humans are in relationship with all the rest of creation.

God and His creation, God and His people, the woman and the man, the human and the creation . . . sometimes this is called the principle of "the great *and*." The universe is built on relationships. In each instance the relationship between the two sides of the "and" is fluid and dynamic, not mechanical or deterministic.

PERICHORESIS, THE GREAT DANCE OF LIFE

The Cappadocian fathers[45] taught the concept of the *perichoresis*, or the great dance of life.[46] Perichoresis is the great dance between God and humans. God may be thought of as the male partner; He takes the lead. He is sovereign, but we are free and responsible partners in the dance.

Pastor Timothy Keller effectively captures this divine dance.

> The life of the Trinity is characterized not by self-centeredness but by mutually self-giving love. When we delight and serve someone else, we enter into a dynamic orbit around him or her, we center on the interests and desires of the other. That creates a dance, particularly if there are three persons, each of whom moves around the other two. So it is, the Bible tells us. Each of the divine persons centers upon the others. None demands that the others revolve around him. Each voluntarily circles the other two, pouring love, delight, and adoration into them. Each person of the Trinity loves, adores, defers to, and rejoices in the others. That creates a dynamic pulsating dance of joy and love. The early leaders of the Greek church had a word for this—perichoresis.[47]

Why do we enjoy an Olympic event like synchronized swimming, or a Russian folk dance, or a ballet? It's a picture of the harmony that God built into the universe. A healthy marriage is another picture of the great dance.

C. S. Lewis, writing at the end of his science fiction book *Perelandra*, uses the same term to describe this cosmic dynamic.

> In the plan of the Great Dance plans without number interlock, and each movement becomes in its reason the breaking into flower of the whole design to which all else is directed. Thus each is equally at the center and none are there by being equals, but some by giving place and some by receiving it, the small things by their smallness and

the great by their greatness, and all the patterns linked and looped together by the unions of a kneeling with a scepter love. Blessed be He!

So with the Great Dance. Set your eyes on one movement and it will lead you through all patterns and it will seem to you the master movement. But the seeming will be true. Let no mouth open to gainsay it. There seems no plan because it is all plan: there seems no centre because it is all centre. Blessed be He![48]

Educator and theologian Greg Uttinger captures the essence of the Great Dance: "The metaphor [of the Great Dance] is apt. In a ballroom dance or a folk dance, each participant is responsible for his own role. He cannot see the whole, let alone shape the whole. But as he dances his part well, as he submits himself to the rules of the dance, he helps to create a thing of wondrous complexity and great beauty. Such is the universe, and such is the church. But the root of this all lies in the inner life of the Triune God."[49] Of course, not only is the beauty of the dance a pertinent metaphor for our life in God, but the pleasure of the dance is another dimension of the same joy. When we are in step with the divine Partner, we experience the joy for which we were created.

In the metaphor of the Great Dance, life is like a piece of music. God is the composer; we are the notes. Each of us has a place, and when all are put together, they create beautiful music. When we know God and follow Him in the dance; we are part of the beauty. When we fail to recognize this, we bring chaos rather than beauty, like someone trying to break dance in the middle of a waltz. If we make God's purpose the purpose of our own lives, then we can join the dance. We can be part of the harmony.

WISE STEWARDS

We have been created to be stewards. God made the human to rule as a steward of creation. We do not own the creation; it belongs to God alone. This is a humbling observation in two opposite directions. On the one hand, as opposed to God the true owner and creator, we are merely stewards. How important to keep in mind the Creator-creature distinction. God is God and we are not! That is an important and humbling truth.

At the same time, we should be humbled by the responsibility God has given us. The God who made everything out of nothing has assigned us to develop His creation, to build on it, to advance it! He made it perfect yet incomplete. He did this with clear intentionality: He wants human beings to "finish" the creation, to make it flourish, to create culture. All this is entailed in the concept of stewardship. We are to be wise stewards of the creation God has provided.

Read

Read Matthew 25:14-30; Luke 16:1-18; Luke 19:11-27.

Identify at least three principles from each parable.

What are the implications for each of these for your life?

We are to function as faithful stewards of the gifts, talents, and abilities God has given us to develop bounty in our communities and nations. We will be held accountable for our stewardship.

Jesus represented Himself as a property owner who was leaving on a journey and met with his servants. "I'm going away for a while. I want you to look after my property while I'm gone." He gave money to each servant in proportion to his estimate of their ability. "Put this money to work while I'm gone," he said. When he returned, he called his servants together to give account of what they had done with the money. "I doubled your money," the first servant said. And the second. But the third said, "I was afraid of you so I hid your money. Here it is." The owner commended the first two servants, but he indicted the third. "You should have at least invested my money and earned some interest."

We will be held accountable for the stewardship God has invested in us. You have gifts, talents, abilities. You have a bounty of capital and God expects you to be a wise steward of that capital. Everyone is a steward; the only question is, will they be a wise steward or a foolish one?

The same applies to nations. A friend of mine (Darrow's) who lives in the Middle East was visited by some Burundians she knew. She was giving them a tour of her country, when they came to a forest in the middle of the desert. Her friends were amazed. The forests in Burundi grow only in rich, black soil. They had never seen a forest growing in sand and rock. They asked my friend to explain this phenomenon. She answered, "God has given every people in the world a land. When He comes back, He is going to ask them what they did with the land He had given them. To my people He gave a desert and wanted to see what we would do with it."

Individuals and nations are stewards of whatever resources God has given them. He expects them to be stewards, to take what He has given and do something with it.

LIFE AND DEATH

Prepare

Read Deuteronomy 30:15-16, 19-20.

What has God set before you?

What are the choices you are faced with?

What does He want you to choose?

What is the relationship between God, His laws, and life?

Wisdom created the universe. Wisdom sustains the universe. Here's another truth that flows from these two: human beings who are wise discover and apply the creation ordinances in personal and national life. It is through wisdom—living within the framework of God's creation—that people and societies become all that God intends them to be. It is folly to seek to live outside the framework God has created. That leads only to death and destruction.

Wisdom leads to life; folly leads to death.

INDIVIDUAL SELF-GOVERNANCE

Wisdom is made for governance. Later we will see the application to civil government, but first let's talk about self-governance.

The foundation of governance rests in the hearts of individuals. All governance begins with internal self-governance or self-control. As professor and historian K. Alan Snyder writes, "All government begins with the individual. Each person is a governor charged by God with the responsibility of governing himself properly, according to His Word."[50] Snyder goes on to list four internal dimensions of self-control: thoughts, attitudes, motives, and emotions.

John Adams was one of the founders of the US and served as its second president. Adams wrote, "Our Constitution was made only for a moral and religious People. It is wholly inadequate to the government of any other."[51] In other words, it is not the external influence or force of a constitution that brings freedom. Even a document as remarkable as the US constitution would be inadequate to direct an immoral, irreligious or lawless people. And no people will ever be moral and religious without self-discipline. Another term for self-discipline is self-governance.

I (Darrow) was in my fifties before I realized this. I remember my *Aha!* moment. I was listening to Dr. Elizabeth Youmans talking about self-governance. Every time she said *self-governance* I translated it *democracy*. That's a form of self-government. But she was talking about something different.

We are to govern ourselves, our own lives. We will either act in wisdom by governing our own lives, or we will act in folly and be lawless. To be stewards of what God has made, we must begin with internal self-governance. I cannot govern outside myself until I have learned to govern myself. Internal stewardship must precede external stewardship. This is what Christian individual self-governance means.

When we govern ourselves on the basis of God's laws, we are free.

Read

Read Proverbs 4:23; 10:5; 6:6-11; 16:32; 25:28.

What do these verses teach you about self-control?

In your own words, describe self-control.

What happens to a person who is not self-controlled?

Over the years I have collected quotes that powerfully illustrate this vital principle of self-government.

He knows not how to rule a kingdom, that cannot manage a Province; nor can he wield a Province, that cannot order a City; nor he order a City, that knows not how to regulate a Village; nor he a Village, that cannot guide a Family; nor can that man Govern well a Family that knows not how to Govern himself, neither can any Govern himself unless reason be Lord, Will and Appetite her vassals: nor can Reason rule unless herself be ruled by God, and wholly be obedient to Him.

Hugo Grotius, Dutch lawyer, theologian, and educator (1583–1645)[52]

Whoever is slow to anger is better than the mighty,
and he who rules his spirit than he who takes a city.

Proverbs 16:32

The Christian principle of self-government is God ruling internally from the heart of the believer. In order to have true liberty, man must WILLINGLY (voluntarily) be governed INTERNALLY by the Spirit and Word of God rather than by external forces. Government is first internal (causative), then extends outwardly (effect).

Dr. Elizabeth Youmans, educator[53]

Men are qualified for civil liberty in exact proportion to their disposition to put moral chains upon their own appetites . . . in proportion as they are more disposed to listen to the counsels of the wise and good, in preference to the flattery of knaves. Society cannot exist, unless a controlling power upon will and appetite be placed somewhere; and the less of it there is within, the more there must be without. It is ordained in the eternal constitution of things, that men of intemperate minds cannot be free. Their passions forge their fetters.

Edmund Burke, English statesman[54]

All societies of men must be governed in some way or other. The less they may have of stringent State Government, the more they must have of individual self-government. The less they rely on public law or physical force, the more they must rely on private moral restraint. Men, in a word, must necessarily be controlled, either by a power within them, or by a power without them; either by the

Word of God, or by the strong arm of man; either by the Bible, or by the bayonet.

Robert Winthrop, speaker of the US House of Representatives[55]

Sow a thought, and you reap an act;
Sow an act, and you reap a habit;
Sow a habit, and you reap a character;
Sow a character, and you reap a destiny.[56]

In Christianity, morality comes from within the individual. This is why, historically, Christianity is associated with political freedom. Those who can govern themselves morally do not need a strong central power to maintain social order.

Gene Edward Veith, provost at Patrick Henry College[57]

God's law must be written on the individual's heart, then later on the stone tablets of the institutions of society.

Grover Gunn[58]

Reflect

Pick one of the previous quotations and do a creative reflection (write a letter, poem, song, etc.).

More recently, a student in one of my lectures put it this way: "When we live in wisdom because of our personal conviction, we become free. On the contrary, we become slaves by the opinions and desires of others. That's the cause and effect." Another student said, "Freedom is not based on my physical condition but on the condition of my heart."

Not long after the fall of Nicolae Ceaușescu, the Romanian communist dictator, I was in Romania. A leader there said something very interesting: "Darrow, for years, we Romanians have been praying that the US army would come to Romania." When I asked him why he would pray for that, he responded, "Because the US army would set us free."

"The US army won't set you free," I said. "You will have freedom when it is born in your heart."

Freedom begins in the heart. An external force will not bring freedom. It must be born inside individuals.

WISDOM LEADS TO THE CONSUMMATION OF THE UNIVERSE

God is involved in history. Actually, that's a deliberate understatement. History is God's story, first and foremost. Humans have a part in it, because God created and loves humans. We speak of "human history" as if it were about us. From our perspective, the story of families and tribes, of wandering nomads, of the development of agriculture and technology, the accumulation of power into ruling clans, the rise of nations, the clash of kings in battles— all the stories of human triumphs and travails leaves us with the impression that we are at the center of the story. This impression is profoundly mistaken. History is God's story, and He is taking it where He will. And at the end of history will come the consummation of all that God has purposed.

When Christ returns at the end of history, He will bring to restoration, fullness, and completion to all that God intended before the foundation of the world. Just as the biblical cosmology describes what God *created*, the Bible also includes a *telos* (Greek for "end," "purpose," or "goal"), that is, the overwhelming *end* of all that God has in mind, the coming of the kingdom of God. The cosmology of creation points to the teleology—the consummation—of creation. In other words, when we look around us and see design in the creation, we are seeing an indication of God's intentions. The design, or form, reveals the function, the purpose for which something was made. The design of an animal's heart reveals its purpose as a blood pump. The form of a bird's wings indicates the ability to fly.

A man in the atheistic Soviet Union once pointed out that a human being can continue learning until the day he dies. He argued that this as an indication of human existence beyond the grave.[59] Consider, for example, that a baby's eyes and ears are formed in the womb, a place without light or sound. This indicates that something lies beyond the womb, something these features have been designed for. The fact that we begin to learn before we are born and continue to learn until the day we die is an indication that there is something beyond the grave.

RECEIVED BY FAITH

Some people stumble when they hear about God directing history in the present. *What about all the troubles in the world?* they ask. Others are dubious about the notion of God bringing history to a grand culmination. In either case, the missing ingredient at such times is the posture of faith, the posture of a finite heart in the face of the Infinite-Personal God.

One example of someone who lived with this faith posture is the patriarch Abraham, deeply revered by all three great monotheistic world religions. About him the writer of Hebrews wrote, "By faith Abraham obeyed when he was called to go out to a place that he was to receive as an inheritance. And he went out, not knowing where he was going. . . . For he was looking forward to the city that has foundations, whose designer and builder is God" (Heb. 11:8–10). This is what drove Abraham into the desert: he was looking for the city of God! He was exercising wisdom, trusting in God's promise.

God, in His wisdom, has created laws and ordinances that will propel creation to its grand finale—the city of God, the new Jerusalem, the coming of God to dwell forever among human beings. It is wisdom that leads to the consummation of all of history. It is the seeking, finding, and applying of wisdom that allows human beings to engage in this grand story. Through wisdom we can discover that order and glorify God by developing our lives (gifts and talents) and our communities, cultures, and countries within the framework of that order.

THE END OF WISDOM–DIVINE GLORY

The end of wisdom is the divine glory. Wisdom created the universe, sustains the universe, and calls men and women to engage in *His* story and the consummation of all history. As we explore creation and the created order, we see more and more of God's glory. God has hidden Himself all around us. He is waiting for the wise person to seek and to find Him. The wise will come to understand the creation ordinances (discover God's thoughts after Him) and know the One who *is* wisdom so their lives and governments will be rightly ordered.

Encyclopedia: The Circle of Knowledge

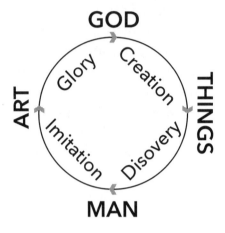

Figure 4

In chapter 1 we included an illustration (see fig. 4). We have seen that

- God is the primary creator;
- man is the secondary creator;
- man discovers God's revelation through the three books: the Bible, nature, and the mind; and
- man's discoveries of God's creation lead to human imitation of God; man develops the raw materials of the creation to produce art, technology, and so on.

David Scott summarizes: "Through scholarship, humankind discovers God's design and forms this knowledge into an imitation of God's design in the disciplines of the arts and sciences."[60] Man's (secondary) creation may be summed up in a word: culture.

As the secondary creator, man reveals the Primary Creator and His creation. As man creates culture, God is glorified and the earth is filled with the knowledge of God. This circle of creation, discovery, imitation, and glory is the circle of knowledge.

This touches on something we mentioned in the previous chapter about the Puritans. In the Puritan vision, the circle of knowledge was the foundation for all education. Vocation is not separated from theological reflection but founded on it. God is on a mission and has called us to join Him. Two mandates describe our mission: the Cultural Commission[61] (Gen. 1:26–28) given at creation, and the Great Commission (Matt. 28:18–20) given before Christ's ascension. These provided a unified field of knowledge, the integrative principle for all education.

The Puritans had an actual educational system design with this unified knowledge in mind. It was called Technologia. The foundation for Technologia was laid by the Moravian educational reformer John Amos Comenius (1592–1670). Technologia was a wholistic curriculum that related work to the context of worldview and first principles articulated in the Scriptures. Its systematic, well-defined, comprehensive structure helped each person learn to glorify God and enjoy Him forever. It created the framework for each person to understand and pursue their own unique, God-given calling. Technologia became the moral and metaphysical "map in the mind."

Reflect

What is one new insight you have gained from this chapter?

How do you want to see this insight applied in your life?

God is the source of wisdom. Wisdom comes from Him. But He has not kept it to Himself. To the humble person God shows His secrets, the wonders of His wisdom. David reflected on this powerful truth:

O LORD, our Lord,
> how majestic is your name in all the earth!
You have set your glory
> above the heavens.
From the lips of children and infants you have ordained praise.
(Ps. 8:1–2)

God invites humans to partner with Him in shaping the world. This truth carries lots of implications. For one, how can humans be equipped for such a responsibility? That's where we will go next.

Part 2

_____

The Preeminence of Wisdom

4

Proverbs, the Guidebook for Life

Prepare

Respond to the following questions.

What is activism?

What is intellectualism?

Identify where you would be on the following scale:

Activism <----------------------> *Intellectualism*

What is the difference between action and "moral" action? Give an example of each.

Some people are wired to be activists. They don't think so much about what they are doing, but they get fully into it. Other people are wired to reflect. They're always thinking, always asking questions.

Activism versus intellectualism—which better describes you?

Everyone is wired in one direction more than the other, but we all need to exhibit both reflection and action to achieve a balance in life and work. You could spend your whole life doing things without thinking, which could mean doing the wrong things. Sometimes people and organizations want to "do things right" and end up doing the wrong things with excellence. We talked about this a lot at the nonprofit organization where I (Darrow) worked.

On one occasion I was teaching about one hundred staff from our Peruvian office. I made the earlier observation about activism and intellectualism and then asked staff to place themselves in the category they identified with. A pure activist was to stand against one wall, a pure "reflector" against the other. Since most people are a blend, I asked them to position themselves between the walls according to their self-perception. Of the hundred people in the class, ninety-nine were between the middle of the room and the activist wall (mostly nearer the wall than the middle of the room). Nonprofit organizations working among the poor are, typically, filled with activists. One young woman stood all alone near the reflection wall, in tears. The class exercise had highlighted the loneliness she had experienced as the only "reflector" in an organization of activists.

In fact, few relief and development organizations attract people who like to reflect. As a result, such organizations often act without sufficient reflection about what they are doing and why they are doing it. They assume, "If we bring money and technology to poor communities, people will escape poverty." Sometimes all that money increases the poverty. But activists who don't take time to reflect will never discover that. And yet people who like to think are slow to get their hands dirty. Their world is all academic.

Neither extreme is desirable, and neither is necessary. We can be balanced. If our nature is to act, we should spend more time reflecting. If our default inclination is to reflect, we need to start doing, getting our hands dirty. In either case, we can have healthier, more fruitful lives by seeking balance.

THE BOOK OF PROVERBS

Three books in the Old Testament are known as Wisdom literature: Proverbs, Job, and Ecclesiastes.[62] Among other features, this genre is marked by two characteristics. First, Wisdom books have limited or no reference to religious life, that is, the temple system, sacrifices, or priesthood so ubiquitous in the rest of the Old Testament. Second, they do not deal with issues related to salvation. Rather, they are focused more on the practical life of a people.

This is true of all three Wisdom books. In this book we are focusing on Proverbs in particular. Proverbs may be thought of as a guidebook for life. It is a book for practical living—street smarts as opposed to academic knowledge. Some people have called Proverbs a very portable handbook for life; it speaks wisdom into all sectors of society. Dr. Ray Lubeck notes that "the patterns in Proverbs are universal. They do not *belong* to God's covenant people."[63]

The Hebrew word for "proverb," *mashal,* means "mental action." This concept could be considered as thought-action. One scholar writes that the word *mashal* has "a clearly recognizable purpose: that of quickening an apprehension of the real as distinct from the wished for . . . of compelling the hearer or reader to form a judgment on himself, his situation or his conduct."[64] Note the pairing of thought ("apprehension of the real") with action ("his conduct"). This is not simply thinking (per the Greek mindset), not the bare intellectualism of knowing the truth. By the same token, neither is it sheer activism, acting without thinking. The Hebrews combined knowing the truth with doing the truth, acting on what is true, good, and beautiful.

The Greeks were famous for wanting to *know* the truth. They didn't care so much about doing it. Many people are like this today. They hear a new insight—perhaps in conversation, or on a podcast, or TV broadcast—and think, *What a good idea!* But the idea never takes root in their life. Or they read a book and are struck with an observation, but never put it into action. They're a lot like the Greeks. They want to fill their mind with knowledge. But the knowledge never pushes through to real-life application.

The Hebrews wanted to *do* the truth. They pursued truth, but not simply to acquire knowledge. They wanted to apply truth to life. One simple definition of wisdom is "the moral application of truth." When we apply what we know to be true through a moral framework, we are using wisdom.

In this postmodern era, many people profess to believe that no such thing as absolute truth exists. There are only individual preferences, only subjectivism ("How does it feel?") or pragmatism ("Will it work?"). This subjectivism is the "guiding light" of most many people in modern life. They have no standard for truth. And if there is no God, and thus no truth, they are correct: there is no absolute right and wrong.

Which leads us to another simple definition of wisdom: making choices to live out truth, beauty, and goodness.

PROVERBIAL FORMS

As is true with every form of literature, writers used proverbs for a particular purpose. A proverb was meant to cause people to think and then to act, to provoke thought and action.

Proverbs take various forms. Many are pithy sayings. Some proverbs come as parables. (Unlike a simple story, a parable has two parts, the fictional story and the reality, i.e., the comparison to which the story is likened.) A proverb may also come in the form of a story, a puzzling statement, or even a riddle. (If you have read *The Hobbit*, you may recall the scene in which Bilbo Baggins and Gollum play a deadly game of guessing riddles.)

All these different forms of proverbs prompt the hearer to reflect, and not just to reflect but to act, even in new and different ways. Proverbs motivate us to rethink our paradigms (i.e., our usual way of seeing things), sometimes to abandon old paradigms and form new ones. We think differently and therefore we act differently. We have an *Aha!* moment.

Proverbs are meant to break paradigms. I often describe parables as hand grenades for the mind. Jesus threw lots of verbal hand grenades. He told parables.

Read

Read Proverbs 1:1–6 (the prologue).

What does the pursuit of Proverbs provide?

Why is it important to study the book of Proverbs?

What is the purpose of the book of Proverbs?

THE PROLOGUE

The book of Proverbs begins with a prologue, an explanation of the purpose of the book.

> The proverbs of Solomon son of David, king of Israel:
> for gaining wisdom and instruction;
>> for understanding words of insight;
> for receiving instruction in prudent behavior,
>> doing what is right and just and fair;
> for giving prudence to those who are simple,
>> knowledge and discretion to the young—
> let the wise listen and add to their learning,
>> and let the discerning get guidance—
> for understanding proverbs and parables,
>> the sayings and riddles of the wise.

Note that the prologue issues four statements of purpose. First, the book is meant for the reader to "gain wisdom and instruction." The implication is that the reader lacks wisdom and needs instruction. Isn't that true of all of us? Even the most educated still have much to learn. Some people are reluctant to admit they have anything to learn, but this is not a sign of maturity. Quite the contrary. I (Gary) heard missionary statesman J. Oswald Sanders relate a story about his wife, now deceased, that illustrates this truth. Ten days before she died, when he was attempting to make her comfortable, she protested, "Dear, don't make things too easy for me. I must keep growing."

The second purpose of Proverbs is "for understanding words of insight." A child learning to read may be very proficient in sounding out the words on the page without understanding the meaning of those words. To understand words of insight means to know how to use the knowledge one possesses. Proverbs not only imparts knowledge; it enables one to understand the implications and applications of that knowledge.

The third purpose is "receiving instruction in prudent behavior." The book of Proverbs teaches us how to live. It is not salvific: it does not teach one how to get to heaven, but how to live on earth. In this way Proverbs is for every human being. It teaches us how to grow and mature as human beings, how to govern our own affairs, how to govern our relationships, our resources, and our communities. People who are wise apply Proverbs in their lives and this leads to their flourishing. People who are foolish ignore and neglect Proverbs to their own detriment and that of their community.

The fourth purpose is "giving prudence to those who are simple." Proverbs exists to help people mature. They help the simple live their lives well, to avoid squandering their time, talents, and resources and instead use them productively. They help young people grow to maturity, learn to discern the times and seasons, and make the most beneficial use of the days they are given.

In short, Proverbs is a guidebook for life!

FOUR THEMES IN PROVERBS

For the rest of this chapter we will discuss four themes of Proverbs that are of interest to our goals for this book. These themes are nation building, common ground, comprehensive application, and basic reality.

Nation building. Wisdom is following God's order, living out God's order in one's personal context. This is the major contributing factor to personal, family, community, and national health, prosperity, justice, and freedom. Where God's order is lived out, we see individual and national flourishing.

Folly is living in denial of God's order. This is the major contributing factor to personal, family, community, and national weakness, poverty, injustice, and slavery. Such descriptors of life clearly indicate that a society is living in folly, denying the truth of God's created order.

Read

Read Deuteronomy 4:1-10. This passage describes God's work of building a free nation from a slave nation.

Identify how the people are to relate to the law.

What will the nations of the earth conclude from watching the model nation of Israel?

Common ground. God created the universe in wisdom; indeed, Wisdom personified testifies, "I was there" (Prov. 8:22). In wisdom God sustains and fulfills the end of history. Because this is true, wisdom is common ground for all human beings. The wisdom of Proverbs creates the bridge between all people who want their lives to function well and to flourish. It is common grace for the entire human family.

Comprehensive application. Wisdom relates to all of life. It speaks to business, family, governance, health care, education, child rearing, the arts, science, and every other dimension of human existence and endeavor. It relates to all spheres of society and all walks of life. Wisdom provides for the enrichment of each person, family, and community.

Basic reality. Perhaps one of the most important themes of Proverbs is that wisdom calls people to reality. Our postmodern world may be viewed as the antireality. Nothing is fixed, all is relative. The concept of absolute truth is rejected; one's "truth" is made up as one goes through life. Beauty has no objective basis for evaluation; it lies in the eye of the beholder. This denies what is clearly disclosed by all three books—Scripture, nature, and the mind—that an absolute standard for truth, goodness and beauty exists. To refuse to recognize this is to be blind.

Such folly would be immediately apparent if people treated other creation laws with the same careless, subjective judgment. Suppose someone were to protest, "Your concept of gravity may be true for you, but that doesn't make it true for everyone" and then act on that foolishness. Of course the suggestion is ridiculous, but it serves to illustrate the folly of abandoning reality in any dimension. All God's laws eventually play out in human life. Gravity is simply more immediate in its effects, not more real. Some consequences take a lifetime to be fully experienced.

Reflect

Postmodernism says nothing is fixed. Give examples of the influence of this thinking.

Give examples of things that are fixed in the universe.

The postmodern view of sexuality has erased many protective boundaries and threatens to dissolve even more. In the West, teenagers are expected to be sexually active; society merely teaches them to practice so-called safe sex. There is no recognition of the sacred nature of human sexuality. Sexual love as designed by the Creator to be expressed in covenantal marriage is reduced to animal urges to be satisfied at a whim. Proponents of so-called same-sex marriage are denying reality, dismantling thousands of years of tradition in every culture of the world. Societies thrive when they honor the Creator's standards for marriage. In fact, the practice of restricting the expression of sexuality to one-man and one-woman marriage is wise. Indeed, this practice has civilized societies.

Dennis Prager, Jewish theologian, writer, lecturer, and radio host, writes, "When Judaism demanded that all sexual activity be channeled into marriage, it changed the world. The Torah's prohibition of non-marital sex quite simply made the creation of Western civilization possible. Societies that did not place boundaries around sexuality were stymied in their development. The subsequent dominance of the Western world can largely be attributed to the sexual revolution initiated by Judaism and later carried forward by Christianity."[65] Marriage provides the woman with security and shelter, a place to nurture children to become responsible adults who contribute to society instead of culprits who cause havoc. It provides the man with a virtuous outlet for his

sexual energies, a God-given remedy to his fallen inclination for sexual pro-
miscuity, a corruption of God's good gift that leads to devastation in a society.
Sexual license in all its forms is foolish and erodes stability—not only that of
individuals and families, but that of communities and nations as well. After
all, the health of the family will determine the health of the nation.

To abandon the Bible's guidance for our sexuality is to descend into
deeper and deeper levels of deviancy, including adultery, homosexuality,
gender confusion, bestiality, and pedophilia. Consider some media offerings
from three societies—the USA, England, and Germany—all of which have
wandered far from their early home in a Judeo-Christian heritage.

- Celebrating adultery—for example, in the ABC television series
  "Scandal"[66]
- Endorsing rape[67]
- Richard Dawkins defending of pedophilia[68]
- Applauding incest[69]
- Mandating a transgender onslaught[70]
- Considering bestiality merely a lifestyle choice[71]

Do you want to live in a world where sexual deviancy is considered
normal? Do you want to raise your children in a society that considers them
sexually available? Who could answer either of these questions in the affirmative? But these are the inevitable end of the abandonment of a biblical ethic
regarding sex.

A society's norms for behavior directly impinge on a related topic dear to
all humans, as seen in the founding documents of the United States. The US
founders enshrined in the Declaration of Independence their understanding
that God has endowed all humans with inalienable rights. Many people profess to agree, and indeed protest with great vigor any perceived encroachment
on such rights, while at the same time denying any absolute standard for
those rights. But without any standards, human rights become meaningless.
A moment's reflection reveals the inconsistency in such a posture.

The attacks of 9/11 were a shock to postmoderns, maybe more than
anyone, in that they powerfully contrasted the position of jihadists with their
own. Real planes flew into real buildings. Real people lost their lives. Like
the sinking of the "unsinkable" *Titanic*, the twin towers—those monuments

to man's ingenuity and technical accomplishment—vanished before our eyes. The attacks were a wake-up call to all of us. To those who want to pretend that their world is what they make it, that reality is individually defined, it's hard to imagine a clearer rebuttal.

Here's another way to illustrate the folly of ignoring or denying reality as an objective standard. Who does not seek medical attention when they are suffering physically? Why do we go, prescription in hand, to the pharmacy and buy medicine? Why do we expect penicillin to be effective? On what basis could such an expectation make any sense other than the fact that penicillin works because God designed it to work?

Wisdom calls people to reality. For life to flourish, people must live within the framework of reality the way God has made it, not in the illusions of what they imagine life to be. When people's lives are broken and impoverished, they often look for a way to make their lives better. Wisdom is the primary means for people to rebuild their lives and communities.

5

Wisdom and Her Brothers

Prepare

Read Proverbs 2:1-6; 5:1-2; 30:1-4 (preferably in ESV, RSV, or KJV).

What three words are found in each of these sets of verses?

Are they synonymous? Why or why not?

How would you compare these three words?

Who's the smartest person in history? Albert Einstein? Stephen Hawking? Marilyn vos Savant? Obviously we could name a lot of smart people. For the most part, we admire geniuses. Who wouldn't want to be smarter, after all?

While intelligence is important, Proverbs tells us that wisdom is more important than intelligence. In this chapter we will explore three related words in Proverbs and the other Wisdom books. If we fail to make a distinction between these words and their meanings, we can become confused. We may be sincere in our confusion, but confused nonetheless.

Throughout Proverbs, wisdom is always related to God. In fact, Proverbs says that the fear of God is the beginning of knowledge and the beginning of wisdom. Proverbs 2:1–6 speaks of the moral benefits of wisdom:

> My son, if you accept my words
> and store up my commands within you,
> turning your ear to *wisdom*
> and applying your heart to *understanding*—
> indeed, if you call out for insight

and cry aloud for *understanding,*
and if you look for it as for silver
and search for it as for hidden treasure,
then you will *understand* the fear of the LORD
and find the *knowledge* of God.
For the LORD gives *wisdom*;
from his mouth come *knowledge* and *understanding.* (Emphasis added)

In this and in other passages, we see the words *knowledge, understanding,* and *wisdom.* The frequent proximity and interchange of these words tempts us to think they are synonymous. But are they? If not, how are they different?

The three words are interrelated but not synonymous. They have things in common. At the same time, they are distinct. In fact, they are hierarchical: they have an ascending order of significance, as we will see.

Knowledge relates to facts, the collection of data and information. One way to grasp what knowledge is about is to ask the question, *What does the data declare?* For instance, let's say you are walking in the countryside and find an unusual stick. You notice that it is about three feet long and an inch in diameter. You pick it up and it feels heavy, from which you ascertain that it is fairly green, recently cut from a tree. This is an exercise in knowledge, the gathering of facts or data.

Understanding has to do with *How can I use this knowledge?* Given the dimensions of the stick, and how green (versus dry) it is, you can gather how strong and flexible it will be. You can assess how it might be used. "This would make a good nightstick," you might think. Or, "I could carve a flute from this."

From there you can apply wisdom. Wisdom asks, *How do I apply this understanding?* The decisions you make based on the data will reveal either your wisdom or your folly. On the one hand, if you decide to use the stick as a club for unjust treatment, that indicates folly on your part. On the other hand, if you used the stick to make a flute, to create beauty, that would reveal wisdom on your part. To create beauty is to imitate God, the Author of all that is beautiful. Wisdom uses knowledge and understanding to develop beauty, truth, and goodness.

Read

Read Proverbs 4:19; 7:23; 24:22; 28:22.

What do these verses reveal about knowledge?

Words have meanings. In fact, most words have a range of meanings. This is true of English (the original language of this book) as well as Hebrew (the original language of Proverbs). Certainly that applies to the terms *knowledge*, *understanding*, and *wisdom*.[72] Furthermore, a word's meaning is shaped by its context, and the nuance can be difficult to preserve in translation. These three Hebrew terms are close in meaning, but the distinctions are important, as we shall see.

KNOWLEDGE

Biblical meanings. The most common Hebrew term for knowledge in Proverbs is *yada*. This verb form (to know) includes noun forms as well, which can mean "knowledge," "perception," or "discernment." This last meaning has the sense of making a distinction: "This hat is red, that one is green" or, more to the point of Proverbs, "This behavior is foolish, that behavior is wise."

Webster's 1828. Webster's 1828 dictionary defines knowledge as "a clear and certain perception of that which exists, or of truth and fact." A person may possess a tremendous amount of data, be able to astound friends with facts, or have the mental capacity to memorize long passages of literature. Yet all this knowledge is of little benefit if they lack understanding or wisdom.

Reflect

Identify someone you know who has a lot of facts, who knows a lot of things.

Is that person smart? Wise?

What is the distinction between being smart and being wise?

With modern technology we have access to a myriad of facts and data. To what end?

Knowledge is rooted in the natural world. Knowledge directs behaviors without consideration of the ethical dimension. It does not give us guidance for life. For example, since the days of Jacob's experiments with cross-breeding his sheep (see Gen. 30), livestock producers have known how to develop hybrids. From those findings, we now have over eight hundred breeds of cattle: Holsteins yield the highest milk volume, Jersey cows give less milk but higher butterfat, Hereford and Angus cattle excel in beef production, Brahman cattle can withstand heat, and so on.

Knowledge is useful, but it doesn't address the ethical questions of life. It doesn't direct us in terms of what we *should* do; it only tells us what we *can* do. And just because we *can* do something (because we have the knowledge and understanding) does not mean we *should* do it. Advances in life sciences in the twenty-first century are just one dimension that screams the question, *we can, but should we?* Some scientists are now experimenting with human-animal hybrids, experiments involving animal embryos and human stem cells. Yes, technological development is part of the cultural mandate,[73] but that is not to suggest that every conceivable technological development is wise. Or good.

UNDERSTANDING

The next level in the three-word combination of Proverbs is understanding. This concept includes building on knowledge, apprehending what is important. It asks the question, what does the knowledge mean?

Read

Read Proverbs 3:5; 16:16.

What do these verses reveal about understanding?

Understanding is an acquired skill. It takes training. We must learn it. Our five senses collect information that goes into our brain. Understanding that information is not as intuitive. However, understanding is better than knowing. Understanding moves us toward discernment.

For example, when you see a painting, you gather information first. You might note the colors, the style (modern, postmodern, the great masters), the artist's name. You are gathering information. You are building knowledge about the painting. You form judgments: *Is it beautiful? Do I like it?*

Understanding takes this to the next level. What movement toward virtue or vice might arise from this painting? Is the artist calling me to what is good? Or is the artist contributing to degradation? Art critics generally regard Picasso's paintings as superb. To be sure, stylistically his work is to be admired. But many of his paintings degrade women. Do you see the importance of applying understanding to our knowledge?

Biblical meaning. The Hebrew term for understanding is *ben*: to perceive, discern; to understand, to know with the mind; perfect understanding. The Hebrew concept of discernment concerns not only ideas but also, in the Picasso example, beauty. I see Picasso's striking stylistic paintings. He is regarded as a master. What can I do with this knowledge? I need to understand that Picasso treated women poorly. He degraded them by his work. To recognize this is to come to an understanding or insight that transcends knowledge. Understanding adds profound value to knowledge. In fact, without understanding, knowledge will be of very limited use. Knowledge will enable me to succeed at planting a garden, repairing a bicycle, or planning a trip. And these are important. But knowledge without understanding seriously reduces the scope and impact of a human life. Understanding moves a person beyond the visible into the vital metaphysical dimension of life.

Webster's 1828. Our dictionary of choice defines *understanding* as follows: "To apprehend the real state of things presented; to judge the truth of falsehood, good or evil." If one knows the truth about Picasso's view of women, beyond the stylistics and the monetary value (determined by the market), one can decide rightly about whether to endorse Picasso's work. As we will see next, wisdom—the moral (or godly) application of truth—raises the question about buying the painting. Why? Because to do so is to support, if not embrace, Picasso's demeaning view of women.

Here's one further insight about the difference between knowledge and understanding. In his essay "Transposition," C. S. Lewis observes how this difference shows up in the animal kingdom. "You will have noticed that most dogs cannot understand *pointing*. You point to a bit of food on the floor; the dog, instead of looking at the floor, sniffs at your finger. A finger is a finger to him, and that is all. His world is all fact and no meaning."[74]

Reflect

What is the relationship between knowledge and understanding?

What does understanding do for information and knowledge?

What is needed for understanding to do its work?

Understanding helps us grasp the meaning or importance of the facts. To translate information into understanding we need reference points of truth.

Years ago my wife, Marilyn, and I lived at Chalet Bethany at L'Abri Fellowship in Switzerland. During that time we had a guest in our home, a physical chemist named Dr. Charles Thaxton. Dr. Thaxton is best known for his work at the Discovery Institute. He coined the phrase *intelligent design*.

One afternoon I went into Charles's room to find him staring blankly at the ceiling. I asked him what was wrong. He said that all his life he had had the answers, but had never had the questions. People with many backgrounds came to L'Abri from all over the world. They came with a variety of questions in their pursuit of truth. In this international milieu, Charles realized that as a Christian he had answers to questions other people were asking but he had never asked. This was an *Aha!* moment for Dr. Thaxton. As a PhD scientist, he had lots of knowledge but did not understand the importance of the knowledge as it practically related to the pressing questions of the day.

For understanding to do its work we need to distinguish between truth and lies, good and evil, the beautiful and the hideous. Many, perhaps most, people go through life without recognizing the importance of making these distinctions. Not every claim to truth is equally valid. Not every assertion of beauty is to be taken at face value. We are often expected to assume moral equivalence between opposing systems as if there were no real difference between good and evil.

WISDOM

All of this brings us to the matter of the moral application of truth. How do we apply truth in our lives?

Read
Read Proverbs 3:19; 8:11; 9:10; 24:3.

What do these passages reveal about wisdom?

Wisdom is active. It does not merely contemplate. Wisdom built the universe. It is God's craftsman.

A friend recently told the following story that illustrates what active wisdom looks like:

> My father's brother, who was ninety years old, just died. He was one of my mentors. At the memorial service one of his grandchildren said that the driving precept of his life, one he lived by and tried to teach his children and grandchildren and all his family, was the commandment "Honor your father and mother and it will go well with you in the land." He wanted his children to know what it meant to go well with them. But honor did not mean simply that you repeat his ideas, but that you lived the kind of life he lived. Kindness to others, not holding yourself above others. His wisdom was active.

Moses prayed, near the end of his life, "So teach us to number our days that we may get a heart of wisdom" (Ps. 90:12). This is a heart longing for active wisdom.

Biblical meaning. The Hebrew word for wisdom is *chokmah*. It speaks of the capacity to understand and to have skill in living, implying adherence to a set standard.

Read
Read Deuteronomy 4:6 and 1 Kings 4:34; 5:7; 10:6-9.

What do these reveal about wisdom?

Earlier we read, "The fear of the Lord is the beginning of wisdom." From this we see that wisdom is rooted in the reverence and worship of God. It begins in the worship of God and moves into action. The queen of Sheba made an epic journey to meet Solomon, considered the wisest man alive. Through Solomon's actions and those of his servants, she saw wisdom displayed. The effect of wisdom was her own newly discovered fear of God.

If we live by these precepts, the nations will see who God is and honor Him.

Webster's 1828. According to Webster, wisdom is "the right use or exercise of knowledge." A related entry says that "prudence is the exercise of sound judgment in avoiding evils; wisdom is the exercise of sound judgment either in avoiding evils or attempting good."

Note the nuance here between the effect of prudence and that of wisdom. The person who exercises prudence avoids harm. If you're walking down a path after a storm and see a branch on the ground, prudence directs you to walk around it and so avoid stumbling and falling. Prudence goes that far: by it we avoid evil. But wisdom goes beyond that and attempts good for others. Prudence goes around the branch; wisdom removes the branch so others also don't fall.

Table 1. Senses, mind, will

Use of faculty	Nature	English	Hebrew	Greek
The senses—what does it declare?	Knowledge—facts and data	Perceptions of what exists, facts	Discriminate, distinguish	Know, accurately recognize
The mind—what does it mean?	Understanding—meaning	Comprehension, conception	Discernment, insight	Mind as a faculty of understanding
The will—how do we apply it?	Wisdom—application	Prudence, discretion	Prudence, skill	Use of knowledge following God's order/design

We have been thinking about wisdom and her "brothers," knowledge and understanding. The table summarizes what we have found. Knowledge answers the questions, *What do our senses declare? What are the facts?* The English word connotes perceptions, which is to say that knowledge deals with what we perceive. The Hebrew term moves this in the direction of distinguishing, making appropriate discrimination between two or more facts.

Understanding takes knowledge to the level of the mind. In other words, having perceived (by sight, sound, feeling, hearing, or tasting) what this fact, or set of facts, means, with understanding we comprehend what we have perceived. The Hebrew word emphasizes discernment, having sound judgment or insight with reference to these facts.

Wisdom is the application of understanding. The English word relates to prudence or discretion. The Hebrew also speaks of prudence and even of skill. Wisdom is practical. It is active. It makes a real difference in one's decisions every day.

Reflect

What percentage of your time is spent on the following?
- using electronics or processing data
- gaining understanding (i.e., using your knowledge to decide what is important and what is not important in your life)
- wise reflection and decision making that will move your life to a state of flourishing

How much do you and your friends think about these issues?

Do a creative reflection (write a letter, poem, song, etc.) on what you have learned about knowledge, understanding, and wisdom.

Why is what you have learned important for your life?

What are you going to do with what you have learned?

6

Wisdom, the Preeminent Sibling

Some well-known ancient Greeks had a lot to say about knowledge, understanding, and wisdom. Aristotle taught about how we acquire knowledge, about the use of the *senses* to examine our surroundings and gather data. Next in importance to this observation is the use of the mind or *reason* to bring order and meaning to the data. This was Plato's contribution.

THE GREAT DEBATE

Raphael was an Italian painter and architect of the Renaissance. His famous painting *The School of Athens* depicts some intriguing details that capture the difference between the views of Plato and Aristotle. Look at the inset (fig. 5) that magnifies the center section in which these two Greek philosophers occupy center stage.

Note their right hands. Plato is pointing upward, toward the heavens. He wanted to understand the meaning of things. His focus was philosophy (as opposed to Aristotle's focus on knowledge through the senses). Plato said that behind each fact is the idea of the thing. Behind the chair is the idea of chair. What's important is not any particular chair but the concept of chair. Plato was the father of idealism. He believed in the transcendent nature of truth, and the related virtue of reasoning. Plato's philosophy included room for a reality beyond the senses, something transcendent of space and time. For him goodness, truth, and beauty are all beyond this world.

Aristotle's hand is extended forward with his fingers held horizontally. By this posture, Raphael was pointing to Aristotle as the father of realism. Contrary to Plato's emphasis on philosophy and meaning, Aristotle taught

Figure 5

the importance of knowledge, the preeminence of facts. From Aristotle the scientific method was born. Truth was factual rather than transcendent. What we know from our five senses comprises what is important. Contrary to Plato's otherworldly teaching, Aristotle was concerned with this world. He cared about the practical nature of truth discovered by the senses. For him the material, "solid" world was what mattered.

For hundreds of years Plato was winning the debate. But with the Enlightenment, the weight went to Aristotle and the scientific method was affirmed. Recall the table from the previous chapter. Aristotle represents the first row, knowledge gained from the senses.

Today our lives are framed by the Darwinian narrative. Every student of Western public education, from grade school through university, has been influenced by evolutionism, the attempt to account for the facts of the universe apart from God. Spontaneous generation seeks to answer the what, but it does not get to the larger questions of metaphysics. In a universe in which

God does not exist, neither does any purpose exist. We are here by accident. There is no meaning, not in things and not in an individual life.

Of course, atheists cannot live with the implications of such a worldview. They live *as if* there is real meaning in their own lives. They act as if love is genuine: they care for their families; they mourn the loss of friends. They also judge people by some kind of ethical standard. They must live this way. Facts without meaning, after all, result in chaos and encourage anarchy. Because no society can long endure anarchy, people turn to substance abuse or amusement to dull their senses against despair.

THEY HAVE EYES BUT CANNOT SEE

Prepare

Read Psalm 115:4-8; Habakkuk 2:18-20; Isaiah 44:9-20.

What characterizes man-made gods?

What is the nature of people who create their own gods?

What does it mean that people become like the god(s) they make?

What happens when technology becomes the thing to which we devote our time and energy?

Many people have perfectly healthy eyes yet fail to make sense of what they are seeing. In other words, they have eyes but they cannot see. They know but they lack understanding.

To see without understanding is very common. At one level we all do it every day. That's because of the human tendency to mentally sort life's experiences into categories, called "paradigms" by some writers. In 1989 futurist Joel Barker produced a training video, "The Business of Paradigms," in which he argued that our tendency to see life in paradigms renders invisible what should be obvious. A scientist, for example, peers at a sample through a microscope and does not see the evidence literally in front of his eyes because it does not fit his preconceived framework—his paradigm—that undergirds his work.

Not only scientists do this. My (Darrow's) wife, Marilyn, worked for many years as a labor and delivery nurse at a Phoenix hospital. One day she was called to the emergency room to assist with a mother in premature labor.

Sadly, the baby was stillborn. The remarkable thing was what happened at the moment of birth. An ER staff nurse, apparently new to obstetrics, exclaimed, "My God, it's a baby!" Of course, every nurse is taught about fetal development. But for this woman the distortion of our modern abortion culture seemed to nullify her education! She seemed to believe that what a woman carries in her womb is "tissue," a "product of conception." She was shocked to participate in the delivery of an actual baby.

Atheist assumptions aside, there *is* transcendent meaning. Truth and goodness and beauty—and, yes, human babies—are real.

UNDERSTANDING

Understanding uses the mind to discover what is important and unimportant. Understanding provides a context for the facts that give them meaning. But, so what? If we understand but walk away without applying the lessons, what good is that?

The book of James uses a fable to picture this. "If anyone is a hearer of the word and not a doer, he is like a man who looks intently at his natural face in a mirror. For he looks at himself and goes away and at once forgets what he was like. But the one who looks into the perfect law, the law of liberty, and perseveres, being no hearer who forgets but a doer who acts, he will be blessed in his doing" (James 1:23–25).

To understand without acting on the insight is to lack wisdom. Wisdom uses the will to lead to choices.

WISDOM

As we have seen, of the three "siblings," wisdom is preeminent. Wisdom uses the will to choose the moral good, to do that which is right and true. It means little to know facts unless you understand what those facts mean. In the same way, and at a more profound level, it means little to have understanding if it is not applied.

The heart of wisdom is doing what is good, telling the truth, and creating beauty. Folly is choosing to do evil, speaking lies, and creating the mundane and the hideous. Wisdom is to choose to live in reality, to live within the cosmic order. Folly is to choose to rebel against reality and try to live in a world of one's own making, a world of illusion.

Epistemological Pyramid

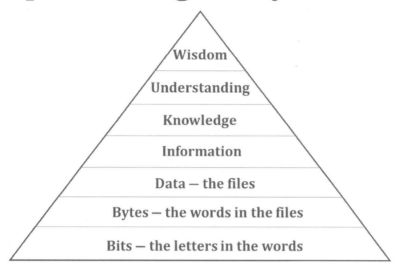

Figure 6

Look at the pyramid graphic (fig. 6). It depicts levels of human knowl-edge. At the bottom, most basic level are the "bits." The word has been used for generations to mean a small amount of anything, but in the computer age it has come to mean the basic amount of information in a computer language (also known as a binary digit). Bits can be compared to the letters in words.

One step up from bits is the "byte" level. In computer language, a byte is eight bits, processed by a computer as a unit. A byte can be compared to a word. Bytes are put together to create files, or data, and data collected is information. Only after that level do we arrive at knowledge, followed by understanding, and finally wisdom.

Reflect

Think about Figure 6 as a grid to gauge where your society is focused.

Which levels do your contemporaries focus on?

Which levels does your church community focus on?

Which levels do you focus on mostly?

It's probably safe to say that in the West today, most of us typically operate at the level of information. We spend lots of time dealing with data. For some, bytes and bits even! We are overwhelmed with information and often unconcerned whether it is true or false. Sometimes our lives are shaped by information only. We spend hours on our computers and handheld devices. We are constantly looking at information, but how often do we ask, "What is the meaning of these facts?" And even more rarely do we come to the highest level, wisdom, to ask, "What am I going to do with this understanding?" We are powerfully shaped by our culture. We have all this data, all this information flow, with little understanding and less wisdom.

Effective pastors point their congregation to Proverbs. What do the facts say? What do they mean? How do we make wise decisions?

Reflect

What are some practical ways in your life this week that you can do the following?
- tell the truth
- do good
- create beauty

THE NATURE OF WISDOM

Prepare

Read Job 28:24; Psalm 139:11-12; Hebrews 4:13; Revelation 2:23.

What do these texts reveal about the comprehensiveness of God's wisdom?

Why might this be important?

Proverbs has much to say about the nature of wisdom. First and foremost, wisdom is sourced in God. One writer has put it like this: "Personified wisdom focuses on God's involvement with the world. . . . The figure of wisdom is the Lord himself."[75] When we read (in Proverbs 8, for example) of wisdom in the first person, we are reading about God. God's rule is universal. It covers all of the creation.

The previous verses could be summarized as, "There is nothing outside God's scrutiny and judgment."

WISDOM IS A MORAL QUALITY

Many people think of wisdom as an intellectual quality, something related to the cognitive or mental dimension of life, perhaps something higher than intellect but in the same category. Not merely intelligence but "brilliance." But if you have read to this point, you will no doubt recognize the error of this assumption. Wisdom is a moral quality. Wisdom moves principles to the practical aspects of life rather than to the abstract or academic.

One way to observe the effect of wisdom in a person's life involves a concept from chapter 1, the cultural trinity. This term is used to capture the three-part model of God's intentions for the creation: truth, goodness, and beauty. We see these three in wisdom. In wisdom's obedience to the moral law we see goodness. Wisdom is also active in the discrimination between the beautiful and the hideous, and between truth and falsehood.

We have written about the difference between smart and wise. When I (Gary) was in high school, we had a school assembly that featured a man who had memorized the entire catalogue of a major retailer, a book about 1.5 inches thick. He passed out multiple copies of this catalogue and urged us to look up any item we wanted and to call it out. He promptly gave the correct page number. We tried everything from bowls to lawn rakes to scissors, but we could not stump him. This was not an object lesson from which he launched into a lecture on some more meaningful subject; this was the entire performance. After about forty-five minutes of this Q&A, the assembly was over. Presumably, he packed up his catalogues and went down the road to the next school! A clearer illustration of the difference between smarts and wisdom would be hard to imagine.

We tend to put wisdom in a category above intelligence. But this is a mistake. Wisdom transcends intelligence. Wisdom is a moral quality. Wisdom shapes practice from a principle. It recognizes truth and applies it to life. It understands the nature of beauty and seeks to create beautiful things and environments. It comprehends what is good and pursues justice. Many people in the academic arena move from principle to abstraction; wisdom takes the principle and applies it.

Have you ever known someone who was wise despite having little formal education? I think of my father-in-law. He was a Nebraska farmer his entire adult life. I was asked to speak for the family at his memorial service. Here's an excerpt:

> Someone has said if you want to know the spiritual state of a man, you only have to look at his family. They are not perfect, just as he was not perfect, but like him his family is healthy, stable, and solid as a Nebraska farmer. . . . That was Bill: a man of integrity, solid, strong, the man you want to have in a crisis. A man who understood the value of people. Look around and you will see the influence of Bill Hansen. Wealth is not counted in gold or stock certificates, both of which will burn up someday. Bill understood that people are what matters for eternity. He invested his life in people. . . . He was a Nebraska farmer and never saw any reason to apologize for that or pretend to be anything else. . . . His friends and neighbors, his children and grandchildren, and his wife of fifty years have much to savor from his life, and they will pass on to others something of the blessing they have received from knowing him. This is his legacy.

Read

Read Proverbs 9:10; Job 28:28; Psalm 111:10.

Where does wisdom begin?

What does this mean?

WISDOM BEGINS WITH THE FEAR OF THE LORD

When you think about it, it makes sense that wisdom would not begin in a mere academic environment, given that it's a moral virtue. So where does wisdom begin? With the fear of the Lord! Reverence of the Creator is the beginning of wisdom.

This is not simply fear in the sense of "afraid of," but more a fear in the sense of "awe, wonder, respect."[76] Fear is a state of piety and respect toward a superior. God is good. His wisdom passes all our understanding. We stand in awe of Him. If we would be wise, we cannot begin with ourselves; we must begin with the One who is bigger than us. Wisdom begins with the fear of the Lord. Wisdom is willingness to live within the reality of the Creator's order.

Read

Read Proverbs 9:10; 14:26-27; 15:33; 19:23.

If you want to be wise, where must you begin?

What does the phrase "wisdom begins with the fear of the Lord" mean to you?

WISDOM IS COMPREHENSIVE

Wisdom touches every area of life. As Creator, God made all that is. He cares for and governs all of life. And, appropriately, His wisdom is comprehensive. Proverbs collects in one book the core of what is necessary to walk in wisdom, to thrive in life.

It is also necessary to see how Proverbs fits in the overall scope of revelation. What is the book's role in God's overarching redemptive plan? The principal author of Proverbs was Solomon, a man of transnational reputation, known as the wisest man alive. Yet, almost one thousand years later, someone would appear and claim of Himself, "Something greater than Solomon is here" (Luke 11:31). What Solomon reduced to writing, Jesus of Nazareth lived out in the flesh. Proverbs summarizes the wisdom personified in Jesus, the one Paul identified as "the wisdom of God" (1 Cor. 1:24).

Wisdom takes insights gained from the study of creation, God's word, and the nature of God Himself and applies the insights to all of life.

We have mentioned Elizabeth Youmans in earlier chapters. Her program, AMO,[77] was developed from an educational philosophy built on the understanding that the Bible is a manual for life. Without that understanding, modern education is built on the lie that there is no God, no truth, no beauty, no goodness . . . life just is. Or, in the contemporary vernacular, it is what it is. Such thinking prepares people to be fools. Those are strong words, but this worldview robs people of the framework they need to be wise. The Bible is the grand story of God and His redemptive history, and it serves as a manual for life, pointing the reader in the direction of wisdom and flourishing. It has the principles that impact and have implications for all of life. "I will instruct you and teach you in the way you should go" (Ps. 32:8).

> ### Read
> Read Exodus 31:1-6; Proverbs 1:1-6; Deuteronomy 4:5-8.
> In what ways do these verses show the practicality of wisdom?

WISDOM IS PRACTICAL

Here's what we find about the practical nature of wisdom. Exodus 31:1–6 indicates that God grants people special skills and abilities. Wisdom gives the craftsman what he needs to design and build beautiful yet functional furniture. This is true for all skills and all forms of human creativity. Wisdom allows us to apply our skills and abilities in ways that lead to human flourishing in our own lives and in the larger community.

WISDOM AND SELF-GOVERNANCE

Proverbs 1:1–6 shows that wisdom bestows humans with ability for effective personal governance. Wisdom provides the average person with the skills needed to succeed in life. To gain wisdom is the most important thing we can do if we would traverse the difficulties of living and thriving in a fallen world.

It was wisdom that led the Puritans to articulate a culture of management that, when applied, created bounty for their community and nation. It was that same wisdom that allowed the Reformers and the Puritans to study Scripture and discern principles of education that led to whole nations becoming literate and educated in Europe and led to the founding of the great universities of the United States like Harvard, Yale, and Dartmouth.

WISDOM AND NATIONAL GOVERNANCE

Deuteronomy 4:5–8 speaks to national governance. Among the nations where God was sending His people, they would become known for their ability to govern well. This would be the gift of wisdom. Those who govern need the wisdom found in God and His order.

Wisdom is fundamental to bringing social peace, justice, economic prosperity, and physical health to the citizens of a nation. Decisions for communities and nations rest on the shoulders of their leaders. If leaders govern foolishly, the nation will wither and decay. If leaders govern wisely, the nation will prosper.

Wisdom applies truth, beauty, and goodness through technical skills and the arts, to the governance of material things, families, communities, and nations. Wherever you see order and beauty, peace and calm, justice and virtue, health and prosperity, you are seeing wisdom applied.

Reflect

How can we, as citizens, influence local and national government to promote wise decisions that lead to national flourishing?

How can individuals use wisdom to make as much change as possible in our own spheres of influence?

WHAT IS MORE VALUABLE THAN MATERIAL THINGS?

Prepare

Read Psalm 119:72, 127; Proverbs 3:13-15; Psalm 19:10; Proverbs 8:10-11; 16:16.

According to these passages, what are some things that are more precious than material things?

What else can you think of that is more important than material things?

Where do today's societies place the most value?

How do you see your culture's values impacting your own life?

Let's think about a needed application of this material on the preeminence of wisdom. Governance—whether of oneself or of a nation—requires discipline. The application of the governance of wisdom will include delayed gratification. How sorely this virtue is needed in our modern Western cultures and their obsession with material things! Too many people live to shop, to go to the mall, to consume. We have to rent storage space for all the stuff we bought at the mall and don't use. Our toys don't drive us to wisdom; they drive us to information.

We go to university, sit in class, and take notes while our professors talk. We are tested to find out how much we remember of what the prof said. But do we have the tools to ask, *Is what he's saying true?* or *What is the meaning of what she is teaching?* We do not have these tools largely because we're not taught to think in these terms.

Often we have trouble as a result of not applying wisdom. We haven't been in the habit of cultivating it. These are real-life situations. They result in poverty in all its forms, and enslavement. They reflect the folly of ignoring God's teaching about wisdom. We do well to heed and follow this teaching rather than ignore it.

7

Worldly Wisdom versus Godly Wisdom

Suppose you invited a group of friends over for a potluck meal. To each one you assigned a dish: a vegetable, bread, salad, and dessert. But when everyone arrived, the salad was not what you expected. You envisioned lettuce, tomato, cucumbers, and shredded carrots. But the salad that showed up was macaroni and relish with mayonnaise. How could such a thing happen? Because *salad* has more than one definition. In this case you intended, "Please bring a green salad," but your friend heard, "Please bring a macaroni salad." Sometimes a word needs elaboration for clarity.

That's what this chapter is about. What is true of *salad* is also true of *wisdom*. What many people think of when they hear the word *wisdom* is very different from what Proverbs speaks of when it uses the term *wisdom* (or, to be more specific, *chokmah*).

Proverbs speaks of something called "worldly wisdom." This references a mistaken view of wisdom. First, let's unpack the idea of worldly wisdom. Then we will speak of the beginning of wisdom as God defines it, and the personification of wisdom.

WORLDLY WISDOM

Prepare

How would you describe worldly wisdom?

How is it different from godly wisdom?

Read Isaiah 5:20-21; Proverbs 17:15; Romans 1:28-32; 1 Corinthians 1:18-25.

What do these passages reveal about the nature of worldly wisdom?

Where do you see this operating in your own culture?

How are you affected by these trends?

When we speak of "worldly wisdom," what are we talking about? Some people use this term as a synonym for *sophistication*, as in, "There's a real debonair fellow. That guy has lots of worldly wisdom." But here we are using the term differently. By "worldly wisdom" we mean human wisdom that sets itself up in contrast with wisdom that comes from God.

Worldly wisdom is an illusion. It doesn't exist in any real way. It is folly masquerading as wisdom. It is a stylish display without virtue, the image of status without purpose. There's no such thing as wisdom apart from God.

Still, the effects of worldly wisdom are very real. Such wisdom leads to destruction. It takes the fool to an undesirable destination. Proverbs shows us this again and again.

GODLY WISDOM VERSUS WORLDLY WISDOM

Already the contrast between worldly wisdom and godly wisdom should be evident. True wisdom is derived from revelation, God's self-disclosure both in creation and in the Scriptures. Here's a further distinction: godly wisdom entails both revelation and reason. Reason without revelation leads to worldly wisdom that ends in impoverishment of soul, intellect, and cultural life. Revelation without reason, on the other hand, leads to anti-intellectualism at best and social tyranny at worst. This is the product of some religions that deny the fullness, or the authority, of God's self-disclosure.

Human beings are the creation of God. They are dependent on God for everything, including wisdom. When humans deny God and build their answers centered on man, their attempts to solve the basic questions of existence, morality, and beauty end in futility. This is another way to say that worldly wisdom leads to illusion. Many people live in a world of illusion.

The apostle John wrote, "If we refuse to admit that we are sinners, then we live in a world of illusion and truth becomes a stranger to us. But if we freely admit that we have sinned, we find God utterly reliable and straightforward—he forgives our sins and makes us thoroughly clean from all that is evil. For if we take up the attitude 'we have not sinned,' we flatly deny God's diagnosis of our condition and cut ourselves off from what he has to say to us" (1 John 1:8–10, Phillips). What does God say about our condition? We are sinners! We are separated from God by our sin. When a person says "I'm not a sinner," they are denying reality and creating a counterfeit reality. They are creating an illusionary world in their mind.

In June 2004 a company called Linden Labs created Second Life, an online virtual world. It bills itself as "a 3D world where everyone you see is a real person and every place you visit is built by people just like you." A new user creates an avatar to represent himself or herself and interacts with the avatars of other users in this virtual world. Second Life has a million active users, and thirteen thousand newcomers join every day. What is most telling about Second Life, in the context of what we are saying about the illusion of worldly wisdom, is that it intentionally promotes the "freedom" of living in a complete illusion. One can only imagine the fallout to real-world relationships, the erosion of virtues such as personal responsibility, the hours and hours of wasted time that accompany such folly perpetuated on such a grand scale.

Relative to the world's population, those who participate in Second Life are tiny in number. But many, many people create a less vivid, but no less dangerous, illusionary world. To deny God or His diagnosis is to create a counterfeit world. Godly wisdom begins with God. When He gives us a diagnosis, we must accept His finding. We don't need a second opinion.

Table 2. Worldly versus godly wisdom

Worldly wisdom _Vice_	Capacity	Godly wisdom _Virtue_
Folly, indiscretion	Wisdom, moral faculty, use of the will	Wise discretion
Disregard, ignorance	Understanding, intellectual and intuitive faculty, use of the mind and heart	Discernment, comprehension, prudence, sound judgment
Heedless, oblivious, unobservant	Knowledge, perception and observation, facility, use of the senses	Attentive, studious, thoughtful

If we want to be wise, if we want to benefit from God's wisdom, our lives must be framed by revelation and reality.

Look at table 2. It captures what we have been talking about. The center column is labeled "Capacity." Starting in the bottom row, it depicts knowledge, understanding, and wisdom, the three terms we discussed in chapter 5. You will recall that knowledge relates to information. We use our senses to gain knowledge. But as the table indicates, the person of godly wisdom responds to information differently than does someone who is worldly wise. The former are attentive to the facts; they are thoughtful and studious. They believe that reality is of God, and therefore all of it is important. They want to examine and understand it. But the foolish (worldly wise) person gives little attention to facts. Such a person is self-focused. Rather than living in awareness of God and His objective reality, they orient their world around themselves. As a result, they are less interested in facts and more interested in feelings. If something doesn't feel good, it has no value. Such a person fails to carefully observe reality. The inevitable result? They bump into the wall of reality.

For example, as children we learn very early about gravity. As we are learning to walk, we fall a lot. We learn to adjust our technique to avoid falling. The same principle applies to other behaviors in which we are often slower to learn. Proverbs says that "pride goes before destruction, a haughty spirit before a fall" (Prov. 16:18). The wise person heeds that instruction and learns humility. But the worldly wise person will continue in pride, only to fall in shame over and over, always falling and never learning. This is what we mean by "bumping into the wall of reality" (maybe we should have said "hitting the floor of reality").

Moving up one row in the table, we come to the level of understanding. This is the use of our intellect, mind, and intuition. We use our intuition and our reason to seek to understand the knowledge that we have. We ask questions like, *What do these facts mean? What do they suggest for the individual? For the community?*

Years ago Christ Hospital in Chicago was performing late-term abortions. Babies who survived were laid in a dirty utility room and left to die. In 1999 nurse Jill Stanek discovered this horror and blew the whistle. Two years later the Illinois state legislature wrote a law prohibiting this action. The law made the hospital responsible to save the life of a baby who had survived an abortion. But the law did not pass. A young state senator led efforts to defeat it. His name was Barack Obama. He went on to serve two terms as the president of the United States.

Were Americans wise or foolish in electing such a person to serve as president? Did they take into account the facts of the abortion legislation? No, they voted their emotion. This is an example of what can happen when people choose to be oblivious to the facts, to reality.

A fool disregards the evidence. He makes decisions without regard to reality. A godly person will be discerning. He will weigh the evidence and will make a sound judgment in relationship to the evidence.

Finally, the third row brings us to wisdom, the moral faculty. In this area we exercise our will. Remember, wisdom lies not in the intellectual arena; it is a moral reality. Thus, a wise person will show discretion in the decisions they make. The foolish person will make decisions either without understanding or intentionally in violation of their understanding: "I know *this* is right but I'm going to do *that*."

How important that we cultivate wisdom in our lives!

Read

Read Isaiah 33:5-6.

What does God do?

What does it mean that He is a rich treasure?

What is the key to this treasure store?

Note: a treasure, treasury room, or storeroom is a storage vault that holds valuables, the figurative extension of blessing and prosperity.

THE PERSONIFICATION OF WISDOM

Prepare

Read Proverbs 1:20-33.

How is wisdom represented?

What does wisdom do?

From where does wisdom call?

To whom does she call?

What are some of the key elements of her message?

What does wisdom provide?

What is wisdom's plea?

What are the consequences of finding wisdom?

Proverbs 8 describes wisdom as if it were a person, a woman in fact. She calls out, she pleads, "Listen to me!" She calls from the streets, the plaza, the crossroads where people walk. She calls to the simpleminded. Why? Because she wants people to flourish.

What does Wisdom offer? She gives truth, safety, security. She builds a strong foundation for good personal governance (see v. 14) and civil governance (vv. 15–16). To listen to Lady Wisdom is to find life and flourishing.

What does the writer intend by this personification? Theologian Susan T. Foh writes, "Wisdom in Proverbs 8:22–31 is better understood as an attribute of God personified. . . . The fact that the noun wisdom is feminine probably accounts for its personification as a woman."[78]

When the writer of Proverbs personifies wisdom, he is calling our attention to the powerful, personal nature of wisdom. It is powerful and personal because it comes from God. God Himself appeals to His human creatures to heed the instruction built into His creation. The personification of wisdom speaks of God's love. Were God an impersonal force or detached divine power, He would not appeal in such direct and intimate terms to humans.

On the other hand, there is another voice that speaks intimately to the same humans, but not for their good.

Part 3

A World of Choices

8

The Twin Choices

Prepare

What does it mean to make a choice?

Think of a book or movie where someone made a choice that changed the whole character of his or her life. What happened?

What are some of the choices you have made that changed the course of your life?

Robert Frost concludes his poem "The Road Not Taken" with these words:

> I shall be telling this with a sigh
> Somewhere ages and ages hence:
> Two roads diverged in a wood, and I—
> I took the one less traveled by,
> And that has made all the difference.

Even if you're not a poetry fan, you can relate to the sentiment. Everyone has stood at a crossroads in life, facing a choice. Should I stay in school or drop out? Should I study or go play? Should I take this job or wait for a better offer? Should I move or stay where I am? Should I seek marriage or stay single?

Life is filled with choices. Some choices are trivial. Some will change your future forever. Wise choices are very important, and Proverbs has much to say about this.

After two months at L'Abri it was time for Marilyn and me (Darrow) to move on. We had planned nine months of travel before going back to Denver. I needed to finish a graduate program, and Marilyn had a full scholarship for a master's degree in nursing. The next two years of our lives were laid out.

But a few days before we left L'Abri, a friend said, "Darrow, have you thought about staying at L'Abri?"

That was easy: "No." But she didn't take no for an answer.

"I think you should pray about staying."

I didn't want to pray about it, but I told her I would. And we did . . . and decided God was directing us through her question. We stayed, and that decision changed our lives profoundly.

Table 3. Two choices

Nature	Portrayed	Practice	Person	Consequences	End
Wisdom	Mother/wife	Virtue	Virtuous/wise	Flourishing	Life
Folly	Whore/ adulterous	Vice	Wicked/fool	Poverty	Death

The book of Proverbs is filled with a series of choices, points of decision between two options. These choices will mark turning points in your life. For example, we read about two women: Lady Wisdom and a prostitute. They have opposite natures: one is a lady, the other is a liar; one is honorable, the other disreputable. They issue from two houses, the home and the brothel. They make divergent calls, one to righteousness and one to seduction. To listen to them is to choose one of two paths, the straight or the crooked. They will lead us to one of two ends: life or death.

Wisdom versus Folly: that choice is woven throughout the book of Proverbs. And yet too many know next to nothing about wisdom versus folly. Even in the church these words are rarely used, and certainly they are not employed in society. We don't use the *words*, and we don't have the *concepts*.

Read

Read Proverbs 2:16; 5:10, 20; 6:24; 7:5; 23:27; 27:13.

How is this woman identified?

What is her character like?

With whom is she contrasted?

We see multiple references in Proverbs to the woman who will lure a man to folly.

> So you will be delivered from the forbidden woman,
>> from the adulteress with her smooth words. (Prov. 2:16)

> Why should you be intoxicated, my son, with a forbidden woman
>> and embrace the bosom of an adulteress? (Prov. 5:20)

> Say to wisdom, "You are my sister," and call insight your intimate friend,
>> To keep you from the forbidden woman,
>> from the adulteress with her smooth words. (Prov. 7:4–5)

> For a prostitute is a deep pit;
>> an adulteress is a narrow well. (Prov. 23:27)

Notice how this woman is identified. She is a forbidden woman. She is not yours. She is an evil deceiver. Her character is described as manipulative, seductive, and deceitful. Her speech is smooth and deceptive. She is hard, selfish, and cunning.

On the other hand, note who she is contrasted with: the woman of folly is the antithesis of Lady Wisdom. She is Madam Harlot, the adulteress. She is wild and untamed.

Sometimes the Bible speaks of adultery in the literal sense. At other times it uses adultery as a picture of idolatry. Worship of a foreign god is sometimes referred to as prostitution and adultery.

"Adulteress" literally means wild, untamed, a woman without boundaries. In Proverbs the adulteress is the seducer, the prostitute. She is thought of in a scornful way that can be summed in the derogatory phrase "that woman."

THE TWO WOMEN: LADY WISDOM AND "THAT WOMAN"

Prepare

Read Proverbs 31:10-31 (Lady Wisdom); Proverbs 6:24-35 (Madame Whore).[79]

What is the nature of each woman?

What is your response to each woman?

Proverbs contrasts two women talking to the same man, each trying to persuade that man to follow them. "That woman" is trying to seduce the man, trying to seduce us. Her intent is to enslave and impoverish. Lady Wisdom is speaking to us as well. She wants us to listen to her and in so doing to live free and flourish. We have a choice. Which woman will we listen to?

Note the character of Lady Wisdom. She is held in high esteem. She does good. She cares for her family. She engages in business to provide for her family. She is a hard worker, generous of spirit, faithful and disciplined.

On the other hand, what is the character of Madam Harlot? The prostitute has very little understanding. She is a seducer, a predator. She looks fragile and delicate but is deceitful and evil. In the animal kingdom, many predators are beautiful but deadly. Consider a cheetah, for example. No one in his right mind would willingly have a predator around. It's not hard to think of contemporary examples of predators. At the time of this writing, Lady Gaga, Madonna, and Justin Bieber come to mind. In other words, this is not an abstraction. The "spirit of the prostitute" is alive today in real people: attractive, beautiful, desirable, seductive. Such people are having a dark and powerful influence on millions of youth.

This chapter personifies wisdom and folly as two women. Can men have some of these characteristics? Yes. But Proverbs is the instruction of a father to his son (see 1:8), warning him about temptations especially powerful in the life of a young man. Thus the repeated metaphor of wisdom and folly as women.

THE TWO HOUSES: THE HOME AND THE BROTHEL

Prepare

Read Proverbs 9:1-6 (House of Lady Wisdom); Proverbs 9:13-18 (House of Madame Whore).

Compare and contrast the two houses.

Lady Wisdom's house is described in Proverbs 9.

> Wisdom has built her house;
> > she has hewn her seven pillars.
> She has slaughtered her beasts; she has mixed her wine;
> > she has also set her table.
> She has sent out her young women to call
> > from the highest places in the town,
> "Whoever is simple, let him turn in here!"
> > To him who lacks sense she says,
> "Come, eat of my bread
> > and drink of the wine I have mixed.
> Leave your simple ways, and live,
> > and walk in the way of insight." (Prov. 9:1–6)

Take a good look at the description of her house. The pillars represent stability. The house is full of abundance so she can give to others. She invites the simple to partake of her feast and walk in the way of insight.

Later in the same chapter we have an account of the prostitute's house.

> The woman Folly is loud;
> > she is seductive and knows nothing.
> She sits at the door of her house;
> > she takes a seat on the highest places of the town,
> calling to those who pass by,
> > who are going straight on their way,
> "Whoever is simple, let him turn in here!"
> > And to him who lacks sense she says,
> "Stolen water is sweet,

and bread eaten in secret is pleasant."
But he does not know that the dead are there,
    that her guests are in the depths of Sheol. (Prov. 9:13–18)

It's not hard to imagine what this house might look like. Rich and visible. Dirty and disorganized. Heavy with the stench of death. Filled with the spirits of evil.

THE TWO CALLS: TO RIGHTEOUSNESS AND TO SEDUCTION

Prepare
Read the following:
Proverbs 8 (the call of Lady Wisdom)
Proverbs 9:1-6 (the banquet call)
Proverbs 7:1-27 (the call of Madame Whore)
Proverbs 9:13-18 (the banquet call)
Compare and contrast the two calls.

The call of Madam Whore is, "Come in here. This is the place to be!" And note two other features of her invitation: she considers herself greater than others, and her call goes directly to the desires of the person.

When your life is guided by passion and feelings, as is true in our culture today, the call of the prostitute sounds inviting. Her voice is sweet, yes. But she is a predator. The fool does not avoid her door. Sadly, today the church is often in sync with the culture. It is reinforcing folly, rather than articulating the need for wisdom; the church, along with the culture, is often simply following feelings to the door of the harlot.

What is the message of Lady Wisdom? Walk in the way of intelligence. She issues a call for prudence, an invitation to weigh carefully the choices before you.

THE TWO PATHS: THE STRAIGHT AND THE CROOKED

Prepare

Read the following:

The path of Lady Wisdom: Proverbs 2:8-9; 2:20; 4:10-13, 18, 26; 6:20-23; 9:6; 10:17; 12:28; 15:19, 24.

The path of Madame Whore: Proverbs 2:18, 4:14-17, 24-27; 5:5-6, 8-10.

Compare and contrast the two paths.

The original language of Proverbs uses two words that are translated "path" in the English. One word speaks of a road and is used metaphorically of our manner or conduct, our way of life. The Hebrew indicates a way of behavior and the destination toward which we are moving.

The other term connotes one's direction, deriving from a literal sense of a well-worn path. Sometimes a hiker is following a trail that can hardly be seen. At other times the trail is easy to follow. When we are walking on the path, our way is clear of obstructions. When we wander from the path, we encounter needless difficulty.

Several years ago I (Gary) was hunting when night fell and I had to find my way out of the woods in the dark. I had followed a trail into the area earlier in the day, but in the dark I could not find it. As a result, I ended up stumbling through fallen timber. In one hand I was carrying my bow. My other hand was gripping a heavy, portable tree stand (a platform a hunter attaches to a tree to gain elevation). In the dark, carrying this equipment, trying to keep my footing through multiple layers of downed trees, I was falling often, scrambling back to my feet, wondering how much further my aching muscles had to take me. It was a frustrating exercise to say the least. I traversed several hundred yards of extremely difficult terrain before finally coming to the road, out of breath and sweating profusely. Only then did I see that I had paralleled the trail just a few yards to my left. What a difference a cleared path makes!

TWO ENDS: LIFE AND DEATH

Prepare

Read Proverbs 1:28-33; 8:32-36; 10:21; 11:1-6.

Describe the "ends" of the two choices.

What end do most people desire?

Are the day-to-day choices people make leading to their desired ends?

Why do people make choices that lead to an undesired outcome?

Life brings us to two paths, that of Lady Wisdom and that of Madam Whore. Two diverse routes with very different ends. That's why it's so important to choose well. The path you take will determine where you end up. One path leads to life, the other to death, one to flourishing, the other to decay.

You choose the path. You cannot choose the consequences, but you can choose the path.

9

Wisdom Lives with the End in Mind

Prepare

Read Genesis 12:1-4.

What did God call Abraham to do?

Where did He want Abraham to go?

What was Abraham looking for?

Read Hebrews 11:8-10, 13-16.

What was Abraham looking for?

How did the people of faith die?

How did God respond to the character of their lives?

Lewis Carroll's well-known fable, *Alice in Wonderland*, includes the following exchange between the protagonist and the Cheshire Cat.

"Would you tell me, please, which way I ought to go from here?"

"That depends a good deal on where you want to get to," said the Cat.

"I don't much care where—" said Alice.

"Then it doesn't matter which way you go," said the Cat.

"—so long as I get SOMEWHERE," Alice added as an explanation.

"Oh, you're sure to do that," said the Cat, "if you only walk long enough."

Alice is in good company: many people seem to care little where they will end up. At least that's the most likely explanation for the unexamined life many people lead. We are all walking on a path, but we may never have considered where the path is leading.

Some people live in the past. (Indeed, there are entire cultures that live in the past.) They are always wishing they could return to an earlier time. "If only I could be young again," they fondly dream. "I had so much fun as a teenager."

Other people live in the future. Still others live in the present.

What time frame do you live in?

Here's a different but related question: Where is the path of your life taking you?

All over the world, many young people are captivated by the shopping mall. They are drawn to the glitzy atmosphere of indoor merchandising. Many families in the West have a vision for a middle-class home in the suburbs. Older people are often longing for retirement, the freedom to go fishing or play golf.

Where is the path of your life taking you?

The ancient Chaldean Abram was living in an animistic, fatalistic culture. Nothing ever changed. From one generation to another, everyone lived in the same village where they were born. Life was on a wheel: it went around and around.

But then one day something happened that changed Abram's life, and eventually the world. It began when Abram heard a voice, a voice that brought him a vision.

"Abram! Abram! I want you to leave. Leave your home, your culture, leave everything you know."

"Where am I to go?" Abram asked.

"I'll show you," said the Voice.

Imagine the ensuing conversation between Abram and his wife!

"We're leaving!"

"Leaving? Where are we going?"

"I don't know!"

No doubt some tension and conflict arose in the marriage. They were probably worshipers of idols kept in their home. Now the one true God was revealing Himself, and Abram's life was turned upside down.

Thousands of years later, a New Testament writer explained what was driving Abraham (as he would come to be called): "He was looking forward to the city with foundations, whose architect and builder is God" (Heb. 11:10).

Abraham was looking for the city of God. This vision was the backdrop of Abraham's life. He was willing to go into an unknown wilderness to find it.

What vision is big enough for your life? Marriage, children, a home: all these are good and proper ingredients of a life blessed by God. Yet none is big enough to comprise the vision for your life. The kingdom of God is the only vision big enough for your life; you were born to serve the kingdom of God. The kingdom of God is the "alternative universe" to the often limited visions of our society and culture.

The wise person lives with the end in mind. He sees the vision and moves toward it. A fool doesn't think about the end. Indeed, a fool rarely thinks at all. He wanders aimlessly. This is not God's intention. He is leading us into the future. We are going somewhere, following the voice of the God of the universe as He takes us to the city of God.

Mark Buchanan, in his book *The Rest of God*, puts it like this: "Wise people ask: Does the path I'm walking lead to a place I want to go? If I keep heading this way, will I like where I arrive?"[80] Too many people are just wandering. By the time they realize their folly, it will be too late. To wander through life is to squander one's years.

> For the simple are killed by their turning away,
>> and the complacency of fools destroys them. (Prov. 1:32).

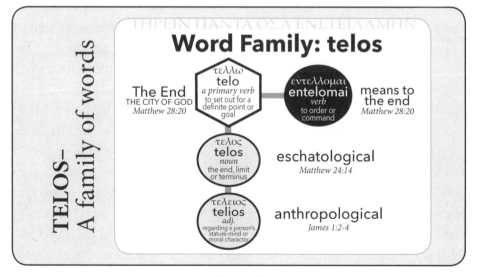

Figure 7

TELOS, A FAMILY OF WORDS

We are thinking about living with the end in mind. What does Proverbs say about that? The Bible frames the concept of ends with the Greek word *telo*, "to set out for a definite point or goal." This term speaks of the end, as in the end of the story, the end of the book, the end of the movie, the end of history.

The family of words rooted in *telo* includes two other biblical words for "end." One, *telios*, speaks of the individual or anthropological end, while the other, *teleos*, is the corporate or eschatological end. Everyone has a personal end, a *telios*, the end for which they were given life. There are two aspects to this end: the general call to life, a summons to all believers, and the unique call for each individual believer. The second concept of end, *teleos,* is the eschatological end. This word means the end of the story, the consummation of history and culture. This is the end for which God made all creation. We find this end described variously: all nations blessed (Gen. 12:3–4), the earth full of the knowledge of the Lord (Hab. 2:14), the wedding of the Lamb (Rev. 19:6–9), the coming of the city of God (Rev. 21:1–4), and the glory of the nations revealed (Isa. 60:1–3; Rev. 21:21–26).

On my (Darrow's) first day of Sociology 101 the professor walked out before several hundred students in the auditorium and asked, "What's the purpose of the life of a child that dies in infancy?" I was nineteen years old. I had never thought about anything like that. I sat there thinking as the professor paced back and forth like a lion ready for the kill. After what seemed like several minutes he came back to the microphone with his answer. "The purpose of the life of a child that dies in infancy is to be fertilizer for a tree."

I was appalled. But I had no answer. Now, over fifty years later, I'm still appalled. Yet I see that he is right, given his assumption of a universe without God. If there is no God, a stillborn child is nothing more than tree fertilizer.

If I saw him today, I would ask, "What's the purpose of your life?" I would insist that, given his view, the same has to be true for him. The purpose of his life is to be fertilizer for a tree! If he is honest, he will see that his assumptions take him to the same place. If the purpose of his life is to be fertilizer for a tree, why is he living? Why is he teaching? If there is no God, what is the end? To fertilize a tree! That's all there is whether one is a newborn baby or a sixty-year-old university professor.

But how many young people go to university and don't even think about questions like this? How many people go through life and never examine their design?

We will all come to an end. How do we get to the right end, the destination for which we were made? That end is found along the path of wisdom. We find it by living in the framework of wisdom, God's law and ordinances. Wisdom is the path that leads to the end for which we were created.

Toward what end is God working in your life? That you be perfect and complete, lacking in nothing. The personal end (*telios*) is to be conformed to God's perfect intentions for your life. This is God's will for every human being.

Table 4. Telios, teleos

Telios—anthropological	*Teleos*—eschatological
Perfect	Coming of the new Jerusalem
Complete	Ingathering nations
Lacking nothing	Kings of earth
Image of Christ	Glory of nations
All God intends you to be	No more death/sorrow

The corporate, eschatological end (*teleos*) is the return of Christ to marry His bride, the wedding supper of the Lamb, and life forever in relationship with our Groom. It is the kingdom come, the holy city, the new Jerusalem. The city Abraham was searching for has come from heaven to earth.

If you are taking your first job, going to university or grad school, moving to another city or country, what path are you on? What will the end be? Are you allowing society to frame your existence, to decide which path you are on?

Read

Read Genesis 12:3-4; Habakkuk 2:14; Revelation 19:6-9; 21:1-4; Isaiah 60:1-3; Revelation 21:21-26.

Identify the images in each of these passages.

What do these images represent?

What is God doing in history?

THE PROLEPTIC LIFE

Prepare

Read Matthew 5:48; Ephesians 5:27; 1 Thessalonians 5:23; 1 Peter 1:6-7; Romans 5:3-5.

What is God expecting of His people?

To what end is He working in each believer's life?

What is the purpose of our trials and sufferings? Let's turn from the discussion of Greek terms to a little-used English word: *prolepsis*. According to *Encyclopedia Britannica*, a prolepsis is "a figure of speech in which a future act or development is represented as if already accomplished or existing."[81] The dictionary defines prolepsis as "anticipation: . . . the representation or assumption of a future act or development as if presently existing or accomplished."[82]

Given this definition of the noun, we can apply the adjective accordingly. To live a proleptic life is to live today in the reality of the future. In other words, we are to live as if the future were present. We are to live in the world we now see, according to what we know is true in the unseen world. "For this light momentary affliction is preparing for us an eternal weight of glory beyond all comparison, as we look not to the things that are seen but to the things that are unseen. For the things that are seen are transient, but the things that are unseen are eternal" (2 Cor. 4:17–18).

We are to live the present in light of future reality. What is that reality? The fullness of the kingdom of God. We are to live today in the reality of the coming of the kingdom of God. Our lives in the *now* are to reveal the *not yet* of the coming Kingdom of God. That is the proleptic life: to live today in the reality of the coming of the kingdom of God.

What does that look like? How would a proleptic outlook change what you are doing today?

WISDOM AND FOLLY

We are to live with the end in mind. So what do wisdom and folly have to do with "the end"?

Both wisdom and folly call us to join them on a path. Wisdom calls us to life; folly calls us to death. Wisdom seeks to discover the end God intended and to walk on the path toward that end, the kingdom of God. Folly, on the other hand, blinds itself to the end. It wanders from the way and finishes at another end. Folly sees no kingdom of God. "Eat, drink, and be merry," Folly calls to us. "Tomorrow you die, so enjoy today. Don't think about the future, don't worry about where you're going."

Proverbs 14:8 states, "The wisdom of the prudent is to discern his way, but the folly of fools is deceiving."

WISDOM SPEAKS

Proverbs 8:32–36 puts things more starkly.

> "And now, O sons, listen to me:
>> blessed are those who keep my ways.
> Hear instruction and be wise,
>> and do not neglect it.
> Blessed is the one who listens to me,
>> watching daily at my gates,
>> waiting beside my doors.
> For whoever finds me finds life
>> and obtains favor from the LORD,
> but he who fails to find me injures himself;
>> all who hate me love death."

Those who love wisdom love life! The fool, however, hates wisdom and thus inadvertently loves death.

E. Stanley Jones (1884–1973) was a Methodist missionary to India whose ministry eventually became international in scope. His twenty-nine books include *The Word Became Flesh*, in which he writes the following:

> I am convinced that we are predestined by the very structure of our beings to be Christian. Note I say "to be Christian," not "to be Christians," for many of us who are "Christians" in the conventional sense are living against the laws of their beings and are thereby being destroyed, maybe slowly, but surely. I believe that predestination is written . . . in our nerves, our blood, our tissues, our organs, our

makeup. It is not merely written in the texts of Scripture, but into the texture of our beings. We can live against that destiny if we desire, for we are free, but if we do we get hurt—automatically. When Christ made you and me and the universe, He stamped within us a way—a way to live. His way; and if we live according to that way, we live; if we live some other way, we perish.[83]

Dr. Jones's language is open to interpretation. He does not seem to be making a theological point about the nature of salvation, but rather an observation about the telenomic principle. The great French biologist Dr. Jacques Monod spoke about "that [which] obliges us to recognize the telenomic character of living organisms, to admit that in their structure and performance they act projectively—realize and pursue a purpose."[84] We were designed by God to be in relationship with Him. We see this in both our design and our function.

Jones is saying that we were made to have a relationship with the living God. That is how we were designed, and that is different from being "religious." God designed us to be in relationship with Him. This design has been built into our nerves, our tissues, our organs. We can live against that destiny if we desire. We can choose another path, because there are two paths. But the path of wisdom is the path we were designed to walk. We have a choice to make.

The two paths have two different ends. Lady Wisdom calls out, "Come, walk on this path. This is the path of life. This is the path for which you were designed. This path will take you to life, to human flourishing." The predator, the whore, says, "No, come to my house." She seduces us to another path, a path we were not meant to walk. We are free to choose this path. But if we do, it will lead to death and destruction, to poverty and slavery.

The fool lives as if history has no meaning. There is no tomorrow; there are no creation laws. Fools live as if their design as a human being has no purpose.

Where do you want to go? If you want to end your journey in the kingdom of God, you will need to pursue wisdom. If you do not care where you are going, you will likely listen to and follow the advice of "that woman."

Reflect

What are your reflections on this chapter?

What are the implications for your life?

10

To Flourish or to Deteriorate?

Prepare

In your own words, what does it mean to flourish? To deteriorate?

Write a list of synonyms for *flourishing* and for *deteriorating*.

Give an example of flourishing and deteriorating in your family, your community, and your nation.

In 1973 Karl Menninger wrote a book titled *Whatever Became of Sin?* Menninger was a famous psychiatrist who saw something happening in US culture. We were losing a word—*sin*—which had long been part of our working vocabulary. As a psychiatrist he was concerned about this. He understood that if the word *sin* was lost, a larger concept—*morality*—would also be lost. He recognized that morality was an important part of human health. As a medical doctor he was interested in the health of human beings. If we could no longer speak with a moral vocabulary, our ability to help people would be substantially reduced. He was mourning the loss in American life of the concept captured in the word *sin*. Menninger was not necessarily a man of faith himself. But he lamented this loss, which has only accelerated since his day.

A shift in a people's worldview is always accompanied by a shift in language. Sometimes the worldview change drives the language change. Abraham, father of the Jews, experienced a fundamental change in worldview that brought a whole new vocabulary to the world. At other times, a worldview shift is driven by an intentional change in language as activists either abandon words (e.g., sin) or redefine words (e.g., marriage) or introduce new words (e.g., autogynephilia, defined at Wiktionary as "the paraphilic tendency of someone who is anatomically male to be sexually aroused by the thought of being a female" and modeled by Bruce, aka Caitlyn, Jenner). In particular, the concern of this book is the language change driven by postmoderns wanting to destroy western civilization and using language as a weapon to do that.

Here's an example. A few years ago I (Darrow) was talking to a group of young women in Puerto Rico who were interested in fashion design. They had observed that clothing choices for women were limited by designers who often had an agenda. These young women were thinking about creating a line of clothing that would be beautiful and modest. They correctly pointed out that the word *modesty* has largely disappeared from our language. And, typically, when the term is lost, the concept is naturally lost as well.

Reflect

Before you change a society, you must change the language of a society. What are some examples of changing language in your society?

Language is important. The words we use shape our thoughts. This is true at the individual level, but it's also true at the level of the society. Language is foundational to both personal and public life. God is the first speaker, the divine communicator. The Bible speaks to us in language, using words. Our thinking about God's truth and God's existence needs to be shaped by the Bible. If the prevailing culture determines our language and our thinking, we are without roots.

Consider some further examples of changes in language. Rather than abiding by the clear designations of *man* and *woman*, we talk about *gender neutrality*. As Menninger decried, we no longer talk about (or believe in) *sin*; now we simply make *mistakes*. And the effect of postmodern thinking means we have rejected *absolute truth* and now believe truth to be a matter of *individual taste*. We have traded *sanctity of life* for *quality of life*. A *baby* is a *product of conception*.

Another effect of the worldview shift in the West has been identified by James Davison Hunter. In his book *The Death of Character*, Hunter shows how the shift in worldview has affected our concept of education. A little over one hundred years ago education was shaped by a biblical mentality. It was purposed for educating young people in knowledge *and* virtue, so they could be wise. As we have moved from the Judeo-Christian worldview to an atheist worldview, our language about education, as well as the very concept of education, has shifted. No longer do we teach virtue; education today is about knowledge and information. Even Christians are framed by this change in concept. Hunter says everybody in North America realizes we have a problem. Our society is increasingly lawless given the loss of teaching virtue. But nobody knows how to solve the problem. Even a man like James Dobson, the founder of Focus on the Family whose international ministry has achieved so much benefit to so many people, doesn't know how to solve the education problem Hunter has identified. We don't know how because the modern world speaks in psychological language.

When America was founded, our language was theological in nature. When we deny God, we move from theological language to a human-centered framework with psychological language. Dr. Dobson, a wonderful champion of biblical virtues, is himself trapped in this psychological language of the culture. Hunter warns of the major difficulty we will have solving this problem. He believes we cannot solve it without a return to theological language. The West has pushed God to the margins; until we return God to the center of life, we cannot hope to succeed.

Hunter's insight provides an important backdrop to our study of Proverbs. When we consider the language of the Wisdom literature—that is, the actual vocabulary—what do we find? How do the writers use language to speak into our lives? Let's consider this question.

The Wisdom literature, including the book of Proverbs, often makes use of word pairs. The writers used opposites to show contrast: wise versus foolish, righteous versus wicked, prudent versus naive, and truthful versus deceitful. Except for the last pair, when was the last time you heard these terms in everyday conversation?

Let's look further at biblical wisdom language that has largely been lost in our society.

Table 5. Flourish or deteriorate

A person's nature	To flourish	To deteriorate
Volition	Wisdom	Foolishness
Character	Righteousness	Wickedness
Discernment	Prudence	Naivete
Integrity	Truthfulness	Deceitfulness

WISDOM VERSUS FOOLISHNESS

The principal Hebrew word for "wisdom," *chokmah*, speaks of "the capacity to understand and so have skill in living. This implies adherence to a set standard." If we consult Webster's 1828 dictionary, we find the following definition for the word *wise*: "Properly, having knowledge; hence, having the power of discerning and judging correctly, or of discriminating between what is true and what is false; between what is fit and proper, and what is improper."

In contrast, the Hebrew term for "fool," *nabal*, means "a man or person who lacks understanding or even the capacity for understanding, implying he is a rebel and disobedient to the law of God." In turn, Webster says that *fool* is "often used for a wicked or depraved person; one who acts contrary to sound wisdom in his moral deportment; one who follows his own inclinations, who prefers trifling and temporary pleasures to the service of God and eternal happiness."

A wise person is described in the Bible as a person who has knowledge, who discerns and judges rightly. A wise person can distinguish between truth and a lie. She can discriminate between what is righteous and what is unrighteous. Not only does she know the difference, she is capable of choosing what is good.

The foolish person, in contrast, lacks knowledge. She can only see what is immediately in front of her. She cannot think of what is eternal and invisible. She is rebellious, willing to disobey the law.

The wise receive wisdom when they obey God. Don't miss the implication: they are teachable! As professor Howard Hendricks said, "A man's teachability is his capacity for growth." Others may be exposed to the same opportunities to learn, but lacking a teachable spirit, they let the opportunity pass without availing themselves of wisdom.

The fool, on the other hand, doesn't want to listen. He doesn't learn from his mistakes. He is self-sufficient and constantly initiates conflict. He brings pain to his parents. He is a cheater who is always guided by emotions.

Read

Read Proverbs 1:7; 12:15-16; 13:19; 17:10; 26:1-12.

List the characteristics of the wise and the fool.

Proverbs speaks of four types of fools: the simple or naive, the mocker, the arrogant, and the rebellious. The simple cannot distinguish between truth and falsehood. The mocker does not respect others. The arrogant is hostile and selfish. The rebellious rejects wisdom, will not accept wisdom. Table 6 further elaborates on these categories and their characteristics.

Table 6. Four types of fools

Type of fool	Characteristics
The Simple (Prov. 1:22)	Naive, easily deceived; cannot tell the difference between truth and falsehood, good and evil, the beautiful and the hideous
The Scoffer (Prov. 1:22)	A big talker who shows no respect; does not take wisdom or wickedness seriously; denies that consequences come from the path one chooses
The Arrogant (Prov. 1:22)	Detests wisdom; openly hostile; lives only for himself or herself
The Rebel (Prov. 1:7)	Loathes wisdom; has nothing but contempt for wisdom; would rather die than submit to wisdom

Reflect

What are ways you have struggled in each of the four categories in table 6?

In which of these areas have you found strength to overcome?

RIGHTEOUSNESS VERSUS WICKEDNESS

The Hebrew lexicon defines *tsaddiq* as "righteous, upright, just, i.e., pertaining to being a person in accordance with a proper standard innocent, guiltless, i.e., pertaining to not having sin or wrongdoing according to a just standard." When we consult Webster's 1828 for the English term *righteous*, we find the following: "Just; accordant to the divine law. Applied to persons, it denotes one who is holy in heart and observant of the divine commands in practice; as a righteous man."

The Hebrew term *resha* means "wickedness, evil, injustice, i.e., a state or condition of evil, with a focus on the violation of moral or civil law by evil deeds; the wicked, the unrighteous, i.e., a class of persons who are evil, with a focus on the guilt of violating a standard." Webster defines *wickedness* as "evil in principle or practice; deviating from the divine law; addicted to vice; sinful; immoral. This is a word of comprehensive signification, extending to everything that is contrary to the moral law, and both to persons and actions."

Evil describes a perverted person who is violating biblical principles. Justice, on the other hand, fulfills the divine commandments in a practical way.

Righteousness brings nourishment to a person's life and to those around them. Wickedness tears others down. One is stable, one unstable.

We need to look for these characteristics in the people around us, the people in our daily lives, and those in government positions. We admire people who are just.

Read

Read Proverbs 3:33; 4:17-18; 10:11; 11:28; 13:5; 17:15; 21:25-26.

List the characteristics of the righteous and of the wicked.

Describe behaviors you've seen that are righteous and behaviors you've seen that are wicked.

Where do you see examples of each nature in your life?

PRUDENCE VERSUS NAIVETE/IMMATURITY

The word *arum* in the Hebrew Bible means "prudent, shrewd, crafty, discerning, sensible, i.e., pertaining to wisdom and shrewdness in the management of affairs, showing a capacity for understanding." Webster says prudence "implies caution in deliberating and consulting on the most suitable means to accomplish valuable purposes . . . . Prudence differs from wisdom in this, that prudence implies more caution and reserve than wisdom, or is exercised more in foreseeing and avoiding evil than in devising and executing that which is good."

The Hebrew term *peti*, "naive" (or "simple" in some translations), means "simple, i.e., pertaining to persons who are easily deceived or persuaded, showing lack of wisdom and understanding, yet having some capacity to change this condition." According to Webster, the English word *naive* is "weak in intellect; not wise or sagacious; silly. 'The simple believeth every word, but the prudent looketh well to his going,' Proverbs 14:15."

We rarely hear the terms *prudence* or *naivete* in today's culture. But Proverbs has much to say about these opposites. A prudent person thinks before he acts.

He looks to the future to consider the consequences of his actions. A prudent person bridles his appetite. He takes precautions to avoid evil. He tries to act on the facts and avoids acting on his feelings. Unlike the naive (or simple), the prudent learns from his mistakes. Webster's 1828 dictionary defines *prudence* as "wisdom applied to practice. Prudence implies caution in deliberating and consulting on the most suitable means to accomplish valuable purposes."

The naive, on the other hand, fail to use discernment. They believe whatever they're told rather than working to find the facts. A naive person walks blindly, going toward his pleasures. As opposed to the prudent, the naive allow their feelings to rule over the facts. They are slow to learn from their mistakes. As an ancient sage put it, they are "like a dog that returns to his vomit" (Prov. 26:11).

A society of people who are captive to their appetites will end in ruin if they do not exercise discipline. Today, for example, we have thirty-year-old "children" still living with their parents and playing video games.

Read

Read Proverbs 1:32; 9:6; 14:15, 16, 18; 22:3.

List the characteristics of the prudent and the immature.

Where would you place the current generation on the scale below?

Prudent <----------------------> *Immature*

What will be the consequences of this reality?

How do these couplets lead either to flourishing or to perishing? Give specific examples.

What does the future your country hold if people lack prudence?

TRUTHFULNESS VERSUS DECEITFULNESS

Prepare

How important is truth in your society?

Give examples of integrity in your society.

Give examples of dishonesty in your society.

In the Bible, the Hebrew term *emeth* means "faithfulness, reliability, trustworthiness, i.e., a state or condition of being dependable and loyal to a person or standard; true, certain, sure, i.e., that which conforms to reality, and is so certain not to be false; honesty, integrity, i.e., being in a state or condition of telling the truth and living according to a moral standard."

The English word *truthfulness*, according to Webster, means "conformity to fact or reality; exact accordance with that which is, or has been, or shall be. The truth of history constitutes its whole value. . . . Veracity; purity from falsehood; practice of speaking truth; habitual disposition to speak truth; as when we say, a man is a man of truth."

The opposite, *sheqer* in Hebrew, means "deception, misleading falseness, i.e., a state or condition which is utterly false and causes a mistaken belief; lie, i.e., a verbal communication which is false; liar, i.e., one who utters falsehoods and lies." Webster defines *lie* as "a criminal falsehood; a falsehood uttered for the purpose of deception; an intentional violation of truth. Fiction, or a false statement or representation, not intended to deceive, mislead or injure, as in fables, parables and the like, is not a lie."

Why does Proverbs commend truthfulness? Why does it warn us away from lying? Because while God wants us to flourish, the liar will languish. He will be broken and punished; he will endure severe consequences. The end of the lie is death.

The one who avoids lies and exercises the truth lives confidently and enjoys happiness. His is an abundant, prosperous life. He hates lying. He knows that lying brings death and poverty. What begins at the individual level eventually manifests itself in every sphere of our society.

Read

Read Proverbs 6:16-19; 12:19, 22; 13:5; 14:5; 21:6.

List the characteristics of liars and of truth tellers.

Has your tongue ever gotten you into trouble? In what ways?

Do these couplets lead either to flourishing or to perishing?

Give specific examples.

11

Virtues and Flourishing

"Only a virtuous people are capable of freedom. As nations become corrupt and vicious, they have more need of masters."[85]

More than two hundred years before Twitter, US founding father Benjamin Franklin wrote that condensed wisdom. He echoes a principal theme of Proverbs: virtues and human flourishing are woven together in the tapestry of human life.

MODELS OF FLOURISHING

We've established the biblical priority on human flourishing. But what does this look like? If God really intended for people to flourish, where can we see that intention demonstrated?

One place to start—a great place, really—is Luke 2:52: "And Jesus grew in *wisdom* and stature and in favor with God and men." It stands to reason that in the incarnate Son of God we would see a picture of His ideal for humanity. And we do.[86]

Luke tells us first that Jesus grew in wisdom. That's what healthy children do. This verse comes on the heels of the account of the twelve-year-old Jesus in the temple. What was happening there? He was "sitting among the teachers, listening to them and asking them questions. Everyone who heard him was amazed at his understanding and his answers" (Luke 2:46–47). As the only God-man, Jesus was unique. But He was truly human, and all healthy children grow in wisdom. In the context, the word *wisdom* can be taken for the various aspects of intellectual growth: wisdom, knowledge, and understanding.

The second dimension of growth indicated here is physical: "Jesus grew . . . in stature." Western societies have an unwarranted emphasis on physical strength and beauty. But that does not obscure the point that physical growth is important in human life. Just because the physical is given inordinate emphasis does not render physical growth and development irrelevant in God's eyes.

Luke also tells us that Jesus grew "in favor with God." Jesus was fully man as well as fully God. While we cannot completely grasp His utterly unique nature,[87] we can accept at face value this affirmation: He grew spiritually. And He grew socially, "in favor with man." At twelve, Jesus had all the normal social sensibilities of a preteen, and the writer records His continued healthy growth in this dimension as well.

Jun Vencer is the former director of the World Evangelical Association. In that role, he taught widely and developed a set of teachings that speak to this fourfold model of human flourishing.[88] He draws from Luke 2:52 to apply these growth dimensions to entire societies. Thus, he speaks of individual and national *righteousness*, *economic* sufficiency for all, lasting *social* peace, and lasting *public justice*, even for the poorest of the poor.

In chapter 3 we quoted Grover Gunn on the relationship between the hearts of individuals and the character of their society's institutions. A relationship exists between a nation's *cultural values* and its *public institutions*. This relationship between culture and institutions directly applies to wisdom and socioeconomic development.

The following observations from Proverbs 16 may be summarized this way: Wisdom guides both individuals and kings. As a king guides, so goes his nation.

> The heart of man plans his way,
> > but the LORD establishes his steps.
> An oracle is on the lips of a king;
> > his mouth does not sin in judgment.
> A just balance and scales are the LORD's;
> > all the weights in the bag are his work.
> It is an abomination to kings to do evil,
> > for the throne is established by righteousness.
> Righteous lips are the delight of a king,
> > and he loves him who speaks what is right.
> A king's wrath is a messenger of death,

and a wise man will appease it.
In the light of a king's face there is life,
and his favor is like the clouds that bring the spring rain.
How much better to get wisdom than gold!
To get understanding is to be chosen rather than silver. (Prov. 16:9–16)

Reflect

What is the relationship between *culture* and social, economic, and political *institutions*?

What is the relationship between *wisdom* and social, economic, and political *development*?

NATIONAL FRAMEWORKS

This connection between individual and national wisdom and behaviors deserves some further consideration.

In the United States we often speak of the "culture wars," that is, the conflict between two or more worldviews which plays out in the public square. In a fallen world, such conflicts are inevitable, maybe even necessary. But the culture wars are generally engaged at the level of public policy. Many people never stop to recognize that politics is downstream from culture. A society's institutions—whether social, economic, or political—are the fruit of the culture. Culture is upstream from politics, and the cult (worship) is upstream from the culture (the manifestation of worship).

Culture is the daily working out of our worship. What does this look like in the institutions of a society?

In an animistic society, spirits are believed to inhabit everything, and worship is made by sacrifices. An offering is presented: a bowl of rice at the base of a tree, incense at a shrine with the worshiper's grandfather's picture. The worshiper burns the incense in hopes that her grandfather's spirit will either look over her or leave her alone.

This worship (cult) directly translates into the institutions of the society. If you need something from a government official, you approach him with gifts (read bribes). You give him an offering to do something favorable for you, or to leave you alone.

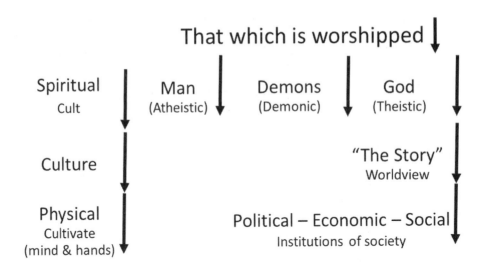

Figure 8

Note figure 8. At the left we see the general principle that the spiritual dimension of human life flows into the culture. Culture is composed of the activities of minds and hearts, and all of that is a reflection of the spiritual. The rest of the graphic shows three alternative systems in which this plays out. Where atheism is embraced, we are seeing the worship of man. Demonic cultures venerate demons. Theistic societies worship God. Each of these three develops a story or explanation of life, a worldview. From that worldview the society crafts its political, economic, and social institutions.

What's inside us comes out as culture; from that we build our institutions. What does this mean for wisdom and human development? Jesus commanded His followers to disciple nations, "baptizing them in the name of the Father, Son and Holy Spirit, and teaching them to obey all that I have commanded" (Matt. 28:19–20). Wisdom is the path toward obeying.

Moral and spiritual development is foundational to national development. This is true at the level of both personal righteousness and public righteousness. The spiritual precedes social, economic, and political development. To pretend that our social mores or economic practices or political establishment can be separated from our spiritual moorings is folly. Every human, and every human society, has some kind of spiritual foundation. Everything else in the life of the individual or society is built on that foundation.

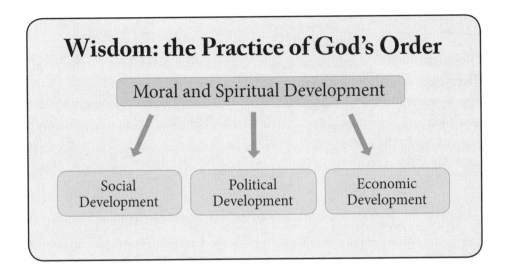

Figure 9

If the foundation is God's order, the result is life. God the Creator built life into the creation principles. His order is life-giving. Wisdom is the practice of God's order.

How can a citizen build a nation unless he begins in himself, his family, his community, his province? The doorway to national life is the heart. From the cultivation of the heart, families are blessed or cursed, communities thrive or languish. The transformation of a nation and society begins in its heart, mindset, worldview, and then moves out into its culture and then into its institutions. This outward growth of the worldview affects poverty in a nation.

God's order is given in the law and in Scripture. By "law" we mean both the personal application of the moral law for righteous living and the public application of the moral law, which is necessary for building just and peaceful societies. Wisdom is the personification of the law, just as Jesus is the culmination of the law.

In the past, the word *Christendom* was used in European and American societies that were largely based on biblical principles. English writer and Christian apologist G. K. Chesterton writes, "If anyone wishes to know what we mean when we say that Christendom was and is one culture, or one civilization, there is a rough but plain way of putting it. It is by asking what is the most common . . . of all the uses of the word 'Christian.' . . . It has long had one meaning in casual speech among common people, and it means a culture or a civilization."[89] Chesterton lived in the early part of the twentieth century. He essentially says that no matter what cultural elements Christians may find themselves in, as they live Christianly, they have a common culture. They are beginning to live in the culture of heaven. That culture is one of truth, beauty, and goodness put into action. Christendom is the Bible taken into the world, not limited to the monastery or kept in the closet. It is Christianity affecting everyday actions, a culture of doing good in a beautiful way that reveals truth.

VIRTUE AND VICE

Let's take this general principle in a more concrete direction. What does a life look like in a society in which biblical principles are acknowledged and followed? One way to characterize such a society is the virtuous life of its citizens. The practice of a limited set of virtues—perhaps two dozen—leads to the flourishing of individuals and societies.

Each virtue also has its corresponding vice that, when lived out, leads to poverty in individuals and societies. Virtues and vices are both inward and outward. They begin in the heart and go out to the sectors of society.

We will examine virtues and vices in Proverbs as they relate to the following:

1. Moral and spiritual development (both personal and public righteousness)
2. Social, political, and economic development

Consider the practice of marriage. From creation, marriage as prescribed by the Creator has been monogamous and heterosexual. In such a context, sexual expression is blessed and humans thrive. Any other expression of sexual intimacy is a vice. When we exercise sexual expression without regard to its virtuous design, we are heading into destruction. This is true for the individual and for the society.

Each virtue and vice is rooted in the Old Testament, stated in Proverbs, and repeated in the New Testament by Christ and/or the apostles. In fact, a life of virtue is fully expressed in the life of Christ. Thus the goal of His followers is Christlikeness.

Read

Read Romans 12:9; Philippians 4:8; Galatians 5:19-23.

What do these passages reveal about virtue and vice?

How are virtue and vice distinguished?

THE BIBLICAL TERMS

Both *virtue* and *vice* appear in our English Bible. *Virtue* in the Old Testament is translated from a Hebrew word (*tehillah*) meaning "praise, adoration, thanksgiving." It is used to "speak positive words about the excellence of another; renown, reputation, i.e. words that characterize a person or people; deeds that are praiseworthy." In the New Testament, the Greek word (*aretē*) speaks of "virtue, goodness, excellence; wonderful act, a manifestation of power, implying excellence." In Webster's 1828 dictionary, virtue is defined as "moral goodness; the practice of moral duties and the abstaining from vice, or a conformity of life and conversation to the moral law." Put simply, virtue is voluntary obedience to truth.

Although there is no actual Hebrew equivalent for *vice* in the Old Testament, a similar and related word (*ra*) is variously translated as "bad, evil, wicked, no good, i.e. pertaining to that which is not morally pure or good according to a proper standard, implying this evil hinders or severs a relationship to a person or principle which is proper." Vice does appear in the New Testament. The Greek word (*kakos*) is translated "pertaining to being bad, with the implication of harmful and damaging—bad, evil, harmful, harshly.'"[90]

We get further help from the early American lexicographer, Noah Webster. "In ethics, any voluntary action or course of conduct which deviates from the rules of moral rectitude . . . any moral unfitness of conduct, either from defect of duty, or from the transgression of known principles of rectitude . . . the excessive indulgence of passions and appetites which in themselves are innocent, is a vice." Our fallen human nature gravitates naturally to vice. Virtues require intentional development. This is the message of Proverbs regarding the nurture and discipline of children.

Virtues are rooted in love.

PREVIEW OF VIRTUES

Earlier we noted that the practice of a relatively short list of virtues can make an enormous difference in the life of a community and nation. In the following chapters we will unpack the virtues in depth. For now, here's a preview.

We will see the application of virtues in four arenas of human development: (1) moral and spiritual development, (2) social development, (3) political development, and (4) economic development. Each of these represents a vital aspect of life that will flourish only as a corresponding set of virtues is practiced. For example, the moral and spiritual development of a community or nation requires citizens who are characterized by seven virtues: meekness, repentance, prayer, hope, joy, righteousness, and self-control.

Our first category, moral and spiritual development, addressed both individual and corporate life. A second category, social development, is especially directed to life in relationship with others—for example, life in families and with friends and neighbors. We will look especially at three family groupings: women and wives, parents and children, and the elderly. With our friends and neighbors, the virtues of love, loyalty, kindness, and peacefulness are of primary value.

The aphorism "charity begins at home" has much to commend it. The practice of virtue needs to be evident first in one's own life and family. When a public servant fails in his private or family life, his suitability for public life and office is profoundly diminished. Having said that, the arena of political development, the third category, lays special demands on the virtues of planning, leadership, and justice.

Finally, the fourth category, economic development, calls for industriousness, thrift, generosity, integrity, and conservation.

Each domain of life benefits from the application of a particular subset of the virtues. Yet all the virtues are always appropriate. In fact, in a sense it's misleading to break these fundamental virtues into separate categories. We do it only for the convenience of study. But all the virtues are fitting in all situations.

Part 4

Wisdom and Development

12

Moral and Spiritual Development

Many nations are in economic decline today. That being so, you might be tempted to jump to the chapter on virtues and economic development. That would be a mistake. Before we can consider economic development (or social or political development), we must ponder the prior question of moral and spiritual development. National economic decline generally grows out of moral decline. Conversely, economic flourishing is often preceded by moral and spiritual development—reformation.

Less than ninety days after the 9/11 terrorist attacks on the United States, another catastrophe of a completely different kind left in its wake a devastation no less profound.

The Enron scandal is one of the most well-known stories of modern U.S. business failures. At one time, some 20,000 people worked for Enron, and many more had retirement accounts largely funded by its stock. *Fortune* magazine awarded Enron "America's Most Innovative Company" six years in a row; company records showed 2000 revenues of $101 billion.

But that rosy picture was inaccurate, and in fact the company was built on systemic fraud. The name Enron is now associated with the term "scandal." In fact, the Sarbanes-Oxley act, designed to protect investors from corporate fraud, was prompted in large part by Enron. Here's one huge irony in the Enron story. Ken Lay, the CEO of Enron, was an evangelical Christian. He attended church on Sunday. On Monday he ran his company by modern business practices without biblical direction. Without a moral framework, the company collapsed and the well-being of thousands of people, employees, and stockholders was seriously diminished.

Indian intellectual and philosopher Vishal Mangalwadi says the collapse of Enron was more significant to the US than 9/11.[91] Why? Because

9/11 was an external attack by foreign terrorists, but Enron is a sign of the moral and spiritual collapse of a nation.

PERSONAL AND PUBLIC RIGHTEOUSNESS

The threat of external attack sometimes lies heavily on a nation's people and leaders. But they might do better to turn their attention inward, to the moral fabric of their own souls. History indicates that nations rot from the inside before they are defeated from the outside. In parallel fashion, to solve an economic crisis, we need to reform culture. The nations must understand and live in the moral and metaphysical framework that supports a free, just, and equitable society.

For example, one of the virtues of Proverbs is thrift, a word hardly known today. Two hundred years ago thrift was a virtue in American life. Materialism was not unknown, of course, but it did not have the hold on culture it has today. People worked hard and saved. These practices allowed the United States to prosper. Today the notion of thrift has virtually disappeared.

Reflect

What is the relationship between culture and a nation's social, political, and economic policy and life?

How do moral and spiritual development relate to social, political, and economic development?

In the previous chapter we listed seven virtues: meekness, repentance, prayer, hope, joy, righteousness, and self-control. A reading of the book of Proverbs will point you to these key virtues for moral and spiritual development. Let's probe each of these in turn.

MEEKNESS

Prepare

Read Proverbs 11:2; 16:18-19; 22:4; 27:1-2, 21; 29:23.

What are the characteristics and consequences of humility? Of pride?

Meekness is often mistaken as a synonym for its rhyme, weakness. That would make meekness the opposite of strength. But this cannot be, of course, given that one Person was both meek and powerful. He said about Himself, "Take my yoke upon you, and learn of me; for I am meek and lowly in heart" (Matt. 11:29 KJV). Others said about Him, "And they were all amazed and said to one another, 'What is this word? For with authority and power he commands the unclean spirits, and they come out!'" (Luke 4:36).

Meekness is a dimension of gentleness, of courtesy. Recall Jesus touching a leper in compassion (Mark 1:41). Lepers were considered untouchable. Jesus had healed at a distance (see Luke 7:3–10); He certainly could have healed the man without touching him. He showed tender gentleness—meekness—by going out of His way to make physical contact with an unclean leper.

Remember Jesus speaking with endearment to Jairus's deceased daughter (Luke 8:54), taking her by the hand and saying, *Okay, sweetheart, time to get up!* No fanfare, no theatrics, just a "simple" resurrection act effortlessly performed in meekness. And how about the time Jesus, in the company of two disciples, arrived at their home village and "acted as if" He was going further rather than assume an invitation (Luke 24:28).

True strength and meekness are intimate friends, not strangers.

Another good example from history is the code of chivalry from the knights of the Middle Ages. They were known for their fierce aspect toward villains combined with a gentle courtesy toward the weak.

Meekness is related to humility. The Hebrew word *tsanua* means "humble, modest, i.e., pertaining to humility and lack of pretentiousness or pride." We get some further light on the meaning by consulting Webster, which has the following entry: "Lowly; modest; meek; submissive; opposed to proud, haughty, arrogant or assuming. In an evangelical sense, having a low opinion of oneself and a deep sense of unworthiness in the sight of God." Without a humble imitation of the divine author of our blessed religion, we can never hope to be a happy nation.

Of course, the opposite of humility, or meekness, is pride. Many people have never considered that pride was the first sin in creation. First, the devil himself, and then the human, fell into the sin of pride. The prophet Isaiah pictures the former in the picture of the king of Babylon.

> How you are fallen from heaven,
> O Day Star, son of Dawn!

How you are cut down to the ground,
    you who laid the nations low!
You said in your heart,
    "I will ascend to heaven;
above the stars of God
    I will set my throne on high;
I will sit on the mount of assembly
    in the far reaches of the north;
I will ascend above the heights of the clouds;
    I will make myself like the Most High." (Isa. 14:12–14)

Apologist and Oxford professor C. S. Lewis made a powerful observation about pride: "According to Christian teachers, the essential vice, the utmost evil, is pride. Unchastity, anger, greed, drunkenness, and all that are mere fleabites in comparison—it was through pride that the devil became the devil. Pride leads to every other vice; it is the complete anti-God state of mind."[92]

A humble spirit in leaders sets a tone for meekness and peace in a society. And in the community. And in the church. Christ followers should be the first to exemplify, as the apostle Paul did, "the meekness and gentleness of Christ" (1 Cor. 10:1).

Reflect

Describe someone you know who is humble.

Why is a humble spirit in leaders so important to building godly nations?

What happens when church, community, and national leaders are proud?

REPENTANCE

If you have ever regretted an action, you have tasted something of repentance. To regret is to feel bad about one's choices. Virtually everyone has regrets. "I wish I hadn't said that to my sister." That's regret. But regret and repentance are not synonyms.

Repentance goes beyond mere regret. To repent is to acknowledge the wrong in the presence of the offended. "I'm sorry I said that to you. I was wrong. Please forgive me." While repentance in human relationships is an essential virtue, it's also important that we approach God with a repentant spirit. God is the divine judge. Every human who has ever longed for justice can be thankful that a judge lives who cares about human affairs and intends to make every injustice right. Where would the world be without a judge? But that coin of justice has another side, one that speaks to the need for repentance.[93] Because God is the divine judge, each of us can only come into relationship with Him in a posture of repentance. We must show a humble readiness to consider God's rightful claims on our lives and behaviors, and we must respond fully to the truth as He makes it known to us.

Read

Read Proverbs 10:23; 14:9; 28:13.

What does repentance require?

In addition to confession of sin, what else will the wise person do?

The book of Proverbs does not include the word *repentance*, yet the concept is clear. Two related words appear in the book. One is *confess*. The Hebrew term (*yadah*) means to "express praise, extol, i.e. make a public confession of the attributes and acts of power of a person; note: there is a focus on the content of praise, spoken out-loud, *usually in the context of the community*" (italics added)—meaning the confession is public, not merely private.

In Webster, confession is defined as "the acknowledgment of a crime, fault or something to one's disadvantage; open declaration of guilt, failure, debt, accusation." Notice that in each case something is amiss in one's life that needs to be acknowledged. It needs to be acknowledged internally, but real confession is taken into the public square. This is a difficult step, but it affirms the genuineness of the repentance.

Both the Hebrew and the English term include this public dimension of confession. Again, we see a parallel to Jesus's use of the term: "Therefore everyone who confesses Me before men, I will also confess him before My Father who is in heaven" (Matt. 10:32 NASB).

The second word in Proverbs which relates to repentance is the verb "conceal." Picture a child who misbehaves in secret. He knows he has done wrong, but tries to hide his transgression. God has given humans a conscience. Even as children, we know when we have done wrong. Proverbs indicates that our efforts to conceal our wrongdoing are foolish and even harmful.

The Hebrew word for "conceal" (*kasah*) means to "keep hidden, *keep to oneself*, not respond with knowledge, i.e. keep information from others, though known and understood by oneself." Wisdom calls for repentance, to reveal what has been concealed.

The term "transparency" gets lots of attention today, and it captures this notion of public confession as opposed to hiding our offences. "Whoever conceals his transgressions will not prosper, but he who confesses and forsakes them will obtain mercy" (Prov. 28:13). Who can forget the Center for Medical Progress undercover videos that exposed Planned Parenthood officials negotiating prices for the body parts of aborted babies . . . and worse?

Christ followers must model in the community and society the practice of repentance and self-disclosure about one's wrongs. They must encourage others to follow suit.

Reflect

What do the Hebrew words for "confess" and "conceal" reveal about their personal or public nature?

What do you think about the concept of public confession?

Who do you know who has confessed in this way?

Have you ever confessed publically? Describe the experience.

We often use the modern term *transparency*. Do you know a public figure in the church or in civil government who is transparent?

PRAYER

All societies have acknowledged and practiced prayer of some kind. The contrary claim of atheists notwithstanding, to be human is to recognize the presence of an Almighty. That being so, a natural next step is to find ourselves asking Him for help. Or thanking Him for blessings. Or interceding His intervention in the life of another. All these are forms of prayer. And prayer is one of the seven virtuous behaviors exhorted in Proverbs.

We've noted earlier in this series that Proverbs is not salvific in character. The great Hebrew themes of the temple, the sacrifice system, and the priesthood are not to be found here. Rather, the writer's concern is how to thrive in the here and now.

Having said that, it's important not to lose sight of the Christological dimension of all the Old Testament, per Jesus's claim, "Everything written about me in the Law of Moses and the Prophets and the Psalms must be fulfilled" (Luke 24:44). Proverbs, for example, whispers throughout of One to come who is Himself "the wisdom of God" (1 Cor. 1:24).

Read

Read Proverbs 15:8, 29; 28:9.

What do these passages reveal about prayer?

What is the contrast to prayer in these passages?

Only three passages in Proverbs relate to prayer. Why might there be so few passages on such an important activity in the book of Proverbs?

What is more obvious in this book is lots of counsel and advice for practical, everyday needs: relationships, work, dealing with authority, resisting temptation, marriage, parenting, avoiding folly, learning wisdom, et al. This focus on earthly life does not reduce Proverbs to a "secular" work, as there is no artificial divide between the sacred and the secular. It retains a strong Godward direction and points the reader to walk in His ways. And the theme of prayer is one means by which the writer commends a godly life.

The Hebrew writers of Proverbs used a term (*tephillah*) that means "prayer, plea, request, and petition, i.e. the act of speaking to or making requests to God."

Our prayer habits are a good indicator of our sense of reliance on God. Besides the actual mention of prayer in Proverbs (3:6; 15:8, 29) some parallel exhortations feed the concept. A good example is the fear of God. We read the phrase *the fear of the Lord* fourteen times in the book. This is another example of a virtue the writer commends for a flourishing life:

The fear of the LORD leads to life,
    and whoever has it rests satisfied;
    he will not be visited by harm. (Prov. 19:23)

Here's a pair of verses that treat two sides of one coin. On one side, we are warned to avoid pride: "Be not wise in your own eyes; fear the LORD, and turn away from evil" (Prov. 3:7). On the other side, we are encouraged to practice humility: "The reward for humility and fear of the LORD is riches and honor and life" (Prov. 22:4).

Noah Webster defined prayer as follows: "In worship, a solemn address to the Supreme Being, consisting of adoration, or an expression of our sense of God's glorious perfections, confession of our sins, supplication for mercy and forgiveness, intercession for blessings on others, and thanksgiving, or an expression of gratitude to God for his mercies and benefits."

A humble posture, a prayer offered in the fear of God, confers immeasurable benefit. Humans go to great lengths to extract precious resources from the earth, but nothing in the ground can match the value of prayer. Gold, diamonds, oil—all these are trivial in comparison. Individuals and nations that learn to live in the fear of God and practice the virtue of prayer unlock a "supernatural" resource far beyond the value of any "natural" resource.

Some of the US founding fathers acknowledged the value of prayer. George Washington said, "I earnestly pray that the Omnipotent Being who has not deserted the cause of America in the hour of its extremist hazard, will never yield so fair a heritage of freedom a prey to 'Anarchy' or 'Despotism.'" (There's a prayer with immediate relevance in 2018!) Benjamin Franklin said, "I therefore beg leave to move that henceforth prayers imploring the assistance of Heaven, and its blessings on our deliberations, be held in this Assembly every morning before we proceed to business." John Adams declared days of prayer and fasting for the nation, as did Abraham Lincoln, who said, "It behooves us . . . to humble ourselves before the offended Power, to confess our national sins, and to pray to the God that made us." Tragically, that sentiment became a casualty to a seeping naturalism in the society.

Reflect

What do you think about Noah Webster's key elements of prayer?

HOPE

Some people may be surprised to see this term included in a list of virtues. We often consider a person's level of hope to be a dimension of personality. Some people are naturally optimistic; others more pessimistic. But Proverbs teaches us that true hope is grounded in virtue. It also indicates that the hope of some people (the wicked in particular) is false. They may feel optimistic, but their hope is groundless because it is rooted in the ignorance and folly of rebellion against God. There's more to hope than temperament, and the Bible certainly doesn't endorse a Pollyannaish approach to life.

> ### Reflect
>
> Do you tend to be an optimist or pessimist?
>
> What is the national mood in your country today? How is that affecting people?
>
> Read Proverbs 10:24, 25, 28; 11:7, 23; 24:11-14.
>
> What do these passages reveal about hope and despair?
>
> Can we have hope even when our circumstances are not good? Why or why not?

The Hebrew word used in Proverbs, *tocheleth*, means "hope, expectation, i.e. a positive future prospect." Our English word, according to Webster, means "confidence in a future event; the highest degree of well-founded expectation of good; as a *hope founded on God's gracious promises*. . . . A well-founded scriptural hope is, in our religion, the source of ineffable happiness." But, like many words, *hope* is variously defined in everyday use. To say "I hope I win the lottery" has little in common with the way hope is generally used in the Bible. Here's a quick review of what Proverbs says about hope.

> The hope of the righteous brings joy,
>> but the expectation of the wicked will perish. (Prov. 10:28)

Everybody has hopes. Hope is universal. But it doesn't turn out the same for everyone. This verse indicates a different trajectory for the righteous and the wicked. For one, the hope leads to fulfillment; for the other, to despair.

When the wicked dies, his hope will perish,
    and the expectation of wealth perishes too. (Prov. 11:7)

Hope lasts only for a lifetime. At that point one either receives what he was hoping for ("Who hopes for what they already have?" [Rom. 8:24 NIV]) or, per this verse, dies without that fulfillment. His hope dies with him.

Hope deferred makes the heart sick,
    but a desire fulfilled is a tree of life. (Prov. 13:12)

During our lifetime, hope leads us toward the future. And it's such a powerful element in the human heart that it builds expectations. When those expectations are not met, when the object of hope recedes into the future, this delay produces a sickness of spirit.

Let not your heart envy sinners,
    but continue in the fear of the LORD all the day.
Surely there is a future,
    and your hope will not be cut off. (Prov. 23:17–18)

God has promised to care for His children. When we live in the fear of God, He guards our future. This exercise of hope in the future is a cure for the problem of envy toward those who seem to have no regard for God and yet prosper.

My son, eat honey, for it is good,
    and the drippings of the honeycomb are sweet to your taste.
Know that wisdom is such to your soul;
    if you find it, there will be a future,
    and your hope will not be cut off. (Prov. 24:13–14)

Author Joe Rigney teases a delightful question and answer from this truth: "Why did God make honey so tasty and sweet? So that we would have some idea of what wisdom is like (at least, that's one reason)."[94] The sweetness of wisdom assures us that God is real and that we can trust Him for a good future.

Do you see a man who is wise in his own eyes?
    There is more hope for a fool than for him. (Prov. 26:12).

Do you see a man who is hasty in his words?
There is more hope for a fool than for him. (Prov. 29:20)

This pair of observations evoke Proverbs 19:18. A young person without discipline—a fool—has little reason for hope, because only a disciplined life of wisdom leads to a better future. And yet such a fool has more reason for hope than does either "that man who thinks he's so smart" (Prov. 26:12, THE MESSAGE) or "the people who always talk before they think" (Prov. 29:20, THE MESSAGE).

Proverbs' teaching about hope fits into a larger redemptive story. The Bible's 160-plus references to hope include the following:

- The ancient reflection of Job: "Though he slay me, I will hope in him" (Job 13:15).
- The reassuring promise to Jeremiah: "For I know the plans I have for you, declares the LORD, plans for welfare and not for evil, to give you a future and a hope" (Jer. 29:11).
- The ultimate prospect of the Christian: "Waiting for our blessed hope, the appearing of the glory of our great God and Savior Jesus Christ" (Titus 2:13).

Reflect

Why is it important to live with a sense of hope?

How does despair impact a community or nation?

What is the grounding of our hope?

JOY

Prepare

Read Proverbs 3:13, 17-18; 15:13; 29:2-3, 6, 17-18; 11:20.

What is the source of joy or happiness?

Who can be joyful?

What are the things that bring God joy?

If we are surprised to see hope in a list of virtues, maybe the inclusion of joy is an even bigger surprise. Doesn't our joy simply reflect our circumstances? If things are going well, we are happy. We have joy. On the other hand, everyone has a bad day now and then, and some people live with impossible burdens and sorrows. Accordingly, they would know little of joy.

That's not how Proverbs treats joy. Rather, joy is the natural consequence of wise living. Joy comes as we follow God's instruction for life. This means that obedience, not circumstance, is the key to joy. Our circumstances may be so dire as to lead to despair. But joy allows us to live beyond them, knowing that the trials of circumstance can lead to a maturity and completeness, a part of the process of our human flourishing.

That observation evokes the New Testament epistle of James, which has been compared to Proverbs. James opens his letter by writing about joy, circumstances, and wisdom, using language that, at points, sounds like Proverbs: "Count it all joy, my brothers, when you meet trials of various kinds, for you know that the testing of your faith produces steadfastness. And let steadfastness have its full effect, that you may be perfect and complete, lacking in nothing. If any of you lacks wisdom, let him ask God, who gives generously to all without reproach, and it will be given him" (James 1:2–5).

Proverbs uses a Hebrew term, *simchah*, which means "joy, gladness, delight, i.e. a feeling or attitude of joyful happiness and cheerfulness; note: in some contexts, this is a response to, or manifestation of, worship to God and *so transcendent even of unfavorable circumstances*." Webster defines joy as "the passion or emotion excited by the acquisition or *expectation of good*; that excitement of pleasurable feelings . . . by a rational prospect of possessing what we love or desire; gladness; exultation; exhilaration of spirits. Joy is a delight of the mind, from the consideration of the present or assured approaching possession of a good."

A study of joy in Proverbs entails considering joy's opposite: bitterness. The Hebrew word, *morrah*, means "bitterness, i.e. the state of misery and mental distress and anguish." Webster's equivalent definition reads, "in a figurative sense, extreme enmity, grudge, hatred; or rather an excessive degree or implacableness of passions and emotions; as the bitterness of anger." Bitterness often becomes an indulgence, which is ironic given that the individual who becomes bitter is hurting himself more than anyone else. For decades, medical professionals have warned that bitterness in a life leads to harmful side effects. A Mayo Clinic article titled "Forgiveness: Letting Go of Grudges and Bitterness" contains an important insight about the relationship between bitterness and joy:

> Who hasn't been hurt by the actions or words of another? Perhaps a parent constantly criticized you growing up, a colleague sabotaged a project or your partner had an affair. Or maybe you've had a traumatic experience, such as being physically or emotionally abused by someone close to you.
>
> These wounds can leave you with lasting feelings of anger and bitterness—even vengeance.
>
> But if you don't practice forgiveness, you might be the one who pays most dearly. By embracing forgiveness, you can also embrace peace, hope, gratitude and joy. Consider how forgiveness can lead you down the path of physical, emotional and spiritual well-being.[95]

As a child, I (Gary) knew a woman—Amanda Friesen was her name—who lived with severe arthritis that left her profoundly paralyzed, her joints and ligaments frozen rigid. She could move only her arms from the elbows down, her eyes, and her mouth. Driving the station wagon he had modified to receive her paralyzed body, her husband brought her to visit in our home. Forever stamped on my memory is the strange sight of him carrying her, stiff as a board, from the car into our living room. My dad folded down our console piano, and Mr. Friesen laid her on it next to our dining room table. She used a mirror to look at us and join the conversation while we ate and talked together. If anyone had a right to bitterness, it was Amanda Friesen. But she always exuded a deep joy. Anyone who spent time with her went away encouraged. According to Proverbs, this is true joy.

Reflect

We are often confronted by difficult events or undesired circumstances.

List five difficult events or circumstances that have confronted you in the last few months.

How have you responded to these situations—with joy or bitterness?

RIGHTEOUSNESS

At one time in the West, virtue (moral goodness) was valued for its own sake. Sadly, that virtue has faded. Now we practice not so much virtue as "virtue signaling," the conspicuous display of a politically correct position to reassure the in-crowd of our bona fides. It's more important to be *seen* as virtuous than to actually *be* virtuous. (Which evokes a question about the virtue of humility!)

While the term *virtue signaling* is new, the concept is not. Consider these words from Jesus: "Beware of practicing your righteousness before other people in order to be seen by them, for then you will have no reward from your Father who is in heaven. . . . When you pray, you must not be like the hypocrites. For they love to stand and pray in the synagogues and at the street corners, that they may be seen by others. Truly, I say to you, they have received their reward" (Matt. 6:1, 5).

Read

Read Proverbs 2:5-21; 13:5.

What is the nature of righteousness?

What is the nature of wickedness?

What are the fruits of righteousness?

What are the fruits of wickedness?

The writers of Proverbs used a Hebrew term for righteousness that means "righteous, upright, just, i.e. pertaining to being a person *in accordance with a proper standard*; innocent, guiltless, i.e. pertaining to not having sin or wrongdoing according to a just standard." Webster's 1828 gives us this English definition: "Purity of heart and rectitude of life; conformity of heart and life to the divine law. Righteousness . . . is nearly equivalent to holiness, comprehending holy principles and affections of heart, and conformity of life to the divine law. It includes all we call justice, honesty and virtue, with holy affections; in short, it is true religion."

In some circles, "righteous" has a negative connotation. If you have the courage to object to some unethical or immoral behavior, you might hear the retort, "Don't be so righteous!" The companion word *pious* has suffered a similar effect. One almost never hears it used in the original sense found in Webster's 1828: "Godly; reverencing and honoring the Supreme Being in heart and in the practice of the duties he has enjoined; having due veneration and affection for the character of God, and habitually obeying his commands; religious; devoted to the service of God; applied to persons." Today, to be pious is to walk around with your nose in the air. Those who cling to their vices are loathe to hear reminders that the universe has moral standards and a perfect divine Judge.

Proverbs knows nothing of this view of righteousness; the writer calls us to practice true righteousness, behavior patterned after God Himself. We are exhorted to this virtue again and again. In fact, its presence or absence in one's life is an important marker of success or failure.

Again, we have further understanding by considering the opposite: wickedness. The Hebrew word here (*rasha*) means "wicked, unrighteous, i.e. pertaining to being evil, with a focus on the guilt of *violating a standard*; guilty, i.e. pertaining to being legally not innocent of a *violation of law*." The English, per Webster, is "departure from the rules of the divine law; evil disposition or practices; immorality; crime; sin; sinfulness; corrupt manners. Wickedness generally signifies evil practices . . . . But wickedness expresses also the corrupt dispositions of the heart."

Of course, that's the condition of every unregenerate heart. We do well to seek to live in virtue, to practice righteousness. And ultimately, to bow to the one perfectly righteous God-man whose perfect righteousness is freely imputed to all who collapse on His mercy. About Him the apostle Paul wrote, "And because of [God] *you are in Christ Jesus, who became to us wisdom from God, righteousness and sanctification and redemption*" (1 Cor. 1:30).

Reflect

We live in a time of moral relativism. What does that produce in a society?

How would a culture of righteousness affect a nation?

How would a culture of wickedness affect a nation?

How do you see righteousness and wickedness expressed in your nation's life?

SELF-CONTROL

Prepare

Read Proverbs 12:16; 16:32; 20:3, 25; 22:24-25; 29:20-22.

What is the nature of a person who is self-controlled? Who is quick-tempered?

What are the fruits of self-control? Of a quick temper?

Our final term in the list of seven key virtues is self-control. Virtuous behavior includes restraint on one's desires. A nation of citizens who practice self-control, who early learn the discipline of delayed gratification, who recognize that acting on every initial impulse is unhealthy for the individual as well as for the society . . . that nation is blessed.

Reflect

What does it mean to be self-controlled?

What is the opposite of self-control?

What happens when the people of a nation are self-controlled? And when they are lawless?

The Hebrew term *arek aph* in Proverbs means "patient, formally, slow to anger, i.e., long-suffering before getting angry." Our English word *patience*, according to Webster, means "having the quality of *enduring evils without murmuring* or fretfulness; sustaining afflictions of body or mind with fortitude, calmness or Christian submission to the divine will; as a patient person, or a person of patient temper. It is followed by or before the evil endured; as patient of labor or pain; patient of heat or cold. . . . Not easily provoked; calm under the sufferance of injuries or offenses; not revengeful."

The opposite term in Proverbs, *qatser aph*, means "quick-tempered, hot-tempered, i.e., pertaining to being angry with relatively little provocation."[96] Webster's identifies it as "feeling resentment; provoked . . . Showing anger; wearing the marks of anger; an angry countenance; angry words."

For a society to be good, just, and compassionate, her people must be good. But we know from both experience and personal behavior that we human beings are not good. Our propensity is toward evil. Self-control is the virtue that tames evil. Unfortunately, self-control is not a virtue in most societies. (And even where self-control is considered a virtue, it's basically impossible for a human to sustain self-control.) In the modern world, self-esteem—feeling good about oneself—is the virtue. *Feeling* good has replaced *being* good. The exchange will have a deleterious effect on our societies.

When our children were small, Marilyn and I would read to them before tucking them in bed at night. One of the books we enjoyed the most was Laura Ingalls Wilder's *Little Town on the Prairie*. Here, in this simple children's story, is one of the most profound illustrations of the concept of internal self-government.

We pick up the story when Laura, Carrie (Laura's sister), and Pa (Laura's father) are visiting the small farm town of De Smet, South Dakota, to celebrate the Fourth of July. The climax of the celebration comes with a public reading of the Declaration of Independence. After it was read, there was a stillness. And Laura discovered what it means to be free.

Then Pa began to sing. All at once, everyone was singing.

My country, 'tis of thee,
Sweet land of liberty,
Of thee I sing. . . .
Long may our land be bright
With freedom's holy light.
Protect us by Thy might,
Great God, our King!

The crowd was scattering away then, but Laura stood stock still. Suddenly she had a completely new thought. The Declaration [of Independence] and the song [My Country 'Tis of Thee] came together in her mind, and she thought: God is America's king. She thought: Americans won't obey any king on earth. Americans are free. That means they have to obey their own consciences. No king bosses Pa; he has to boss himself. Why (she thought), when I'm a little older, Pa and Ma will stop telling me what to do, and there isn't anyone else who has a right to give me orders. I will have to make myself be good.

Her whole mind seemed to be lighted up by that thought. This is what it means to be free. It means you have to be good. "Our father's God, author of liberty . . ." The laws of Nature and of Nature's God endow you with the right to life and liberty. Then you have to keep the laws of God, for God's law is the only thing that gives you a right to be free.[97]

How beautiful and simple a little girl's reasoning! God is our King. We are to internally govern ourselves by His laws if we are to do good and live free.

For societies to flourish, they must focus on the character of her citizens. People who govern themselves on God's laws and principles are virtuous citizens. Virtuous citizens lead to healthy and prospering societies. Societies that do not work to develop the character of their people will witness decay. Bankruptcy in the character of a nation's citizens will end in economic bankruptcy as well.

Reflect

Wisdom leads to the virtue of self-control. The foolish are hotheaded, quick-tempered. How has a quick temper or anger impacted your life or relationships?

Do one of the following:

- Write a paragraph or two on (1) the importance of personal and public righteousness for the flourishing of individuals, communities, and nations, or (2) how the practice of the personal virtues of meekness, repentance, prayer, hope, joy, righteousness, and self-control contribute to the public righteousness of the nation.
- Do a creative reflection (write a letter, poem, song, etc.) on what you have learned about personal or public righteousness.

13

Social Development

Families

We have written repeatedly about wisdom as the practice of God's order. Wisdom is a way of life. Wisdom is governing our appetites and living our days according to the design that God built into the creation. Thus, wisdom is not an intellectual quality. It's a moral quality. This is one reason the word *wisdom* has disappeared from our vocabulary. Where God is considered absent, an atheistic framework governs everything about life, including language. All is relative; there is no moral framework; we do what is right in our own eyes. Such an arrangement leaves no place for wisdom. In a society where morality is entirely relative and virtue is either mocked or ignored, what can "wisdom" mean?

Yet wisdom benefits any society that recognizes truth and orders life accordingly. The rest of this book will apply wisdom to three areas of human flourishing. This chapter and the next will deal with social development. In

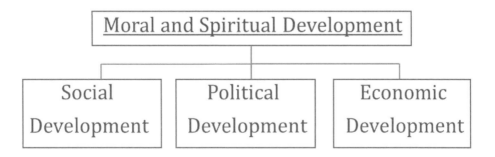

Figure 10

chapter 15 we will consider political development, including planning, leadership, and justice. Finally, we will turn to economic development—the cultivation of industriousness, thrift, generosity, integrity, and conservation.

SOCIAL DEVELOPMENT

Social development in human life has multiple fronts. Proverbs is concerned with four in particular. Under the rubric of family, we see teaching on women and wives,[98] parents and children, and the elderly. Chapter 14 will deal with the fourth context of social development in Proverbs: friends and neighbors.

Modern feminism roared into the West in the 1960s. Helen Reddy's 1971 hit song "I Am Woman" captured the energy and enthusiasm of a generation determined to wipe out injustices, both real and perceived, bound up in the conventional roles of male and female life. My (Darrow) book *Nurturing the Nations* addresses the implications at length.[99] But any study on Proverbs cannot fail to note the special place the writer gives to women and women's concerns.

God differentiated humanity into two sexes; women and men are God's idea. He conceived of feminine and masculine and created them male and female. We are made male and female in the image of God, because the concept and reality of the family is God's idea. So is sex, for the procreation of families. The task given to the man and the woman is to populate the earth with image bearers of God. We read in Genesis 1:28, "Be fruitful and multiply, fill the earth." Genesis 1:16 and 1:28b could be paraphrased, "Create families who are responsible to be stewards of creation and to be co-creators who fashion God-honoring culture." As the book of Proverbs reminds us, the family is the classroom for the education of those who will govern the future. The father and mother are the primary teachers of their sons and daughters. Proverbs is a tool to prepare children to govern the gifts of God: language, numbers, wood, metals, paints, musical notes—all to create culture and invent whole new worlds of imagination.

WOMEN AND WIVES

Proverbs gives much attention to the power of a woman in human life. A woman's capacity to bring flourishing and blessing to society, and her power to bring harm: both are given considerable space in this Wisdom book. We see a woman's power for good or evil, both in society in general and in marriage.

Proverbs 31 provides a glimpse of the nature of a godly woman as well as a comprehensive range of skill sets. The chapter describes the "ideal woman," the high bar of what a woman may achieve. Women can be overwhelmed as they read this description. But here we see the full scope of female potential. These verses may be divided into two broad categories: the character of a godly woman, and a picture of the myriad skills a godly woman may pursue and possess.

We live at a time in history where people's skills count for more than their character. In fact, looking at lifestyles and behavior in today's world reveals that godly character is often disregarded. But, for people to flourish, character is more basic than skills. And a virtuous people will create a prosperous society. So we examine the virtue of a godly woman first.

Note the comprehensive character qualities of a godly woman:

- *A good reputation.* She brings honor to her husband.
- *A robust work ethic.* She is industrious and productive. She redeems the precious commodity of time.
- *Thrift.* She has delayed gratification, saving money for the future.
- *Patience.* She has perseverance in difficult circumstance and is tolerant of people with whom she may not agree.
- *Disciplined physical habits.* She takes care of her body; she is strong and vigorous.
- *Foresight.* She is prepared for any eventuality.
- *Compassion.* She sees and cares for the needy.
- *A lover of beauty.* She cares about aesthetics; her life reflects the beauty of God.
- *Strength of character.* She has deep convictions and lives by them.
- *A woman of dignity.* She is respectful and worthy of respect.
- *Courage toward the future.* She faces the future with calm assurance.
- *Wisdom.* She is characterized by thoughtful behavior appropriate to the situation.
- *The fear of the Lord.* God's opinion matters to her more than the opinions of others or material riches.

Here is a model of virtue. As with Wisdom herself, here godly character is more precious than rubies. Of secondary importance to a woman's character are her comprehensive set of skills. Note that some of these skills come naturally and some are acquired. These skills allow her to fully engage in the cultural mandate of Genesis 1, making her a suitable companion for her husband as a vice-regent of creation.

She is able to do the following:

- select raw materials for manufacturing
- manage logistics and transportation
- provide food for her family and members of her household
- evaluate, buy, and sell real estate
- invest with an eye to the future
- make a profit in her investments
- make cloth and clothing
- merchandise effectively
- teach faithfully
- manage her household

Here is a woman who is a leader and influencer. She cares for her family, the people of her household, even the poor and the stranger. She does her husband good and not harm. Her reputation goes before her, and she is spoken well of. This woman is not a servile, inferior being, slavishly bowing before men. She is a person of dignity, the complementary equal of a man. Ours is not a man's world. It is God's world, designed to be stewarded and developed by the female and male of the human species.

When a group of young people were asked to reflect on what Proverbs says about a virtuous woman, they came up with the following observations:[100]

- She is prudent, careful, patient, and calm.
- She brings energy to the world around her.
- She forgives; she is kind and easy to love.
- She speaks truth; her words are not vain.
- She is sensitive, modest in her dress, graceful in speech and motion.
- She is represented by a flower: we can see the beauty and character of God in the godly woman.

- She is delicate yet a hard worker.
- She looks for what's good for everyone.
- She is a good administrator.
- A man should honor and appreciate a woman like this.

On the other hand, the ungodly woman is seductive. She forgets her covenant with God, roaming everywhere, living and dressing immodestly. In short, she feels she has the right to do whatever she wants.

Proverbs talks about womanhood in marriage as well. The book treats at length the topic of what a wife brings to a marriage, for good or bad. The same group of young people made the following observations from Proverbs about the wife.

- She is a hard worker.
- She has balance: she takes care of her family but also herself.
- The love of God is reflected through her; she is a gift from God for man.
- She loves her family and her husband.
- A godly wife is the crown of her husband.
- She brings beauty to the home.
- The man should honor, admire, and care for her. He should be thankful for her.
- A woman who is not a good wife is not virtuous. She may be unfaithful or hard to live with. A nagging, argumentative wife is a pain to her husband.

Before going further it is wise to make a few distinctions. The Hebrew and the English both make a distinction between two modalities of being made in the image of God, of being human. The language in English is "male and female." In Hebrew (Gen. 1:27), the generic human being is *adam*. Adam comes in two distinct modalities: (1) *zakar*—male, man, that is, the gender of a species that is not female, with no focus on the age or stage in life and female; and (2) *naqab*—woman, female, that is, the biological female of a species in creation, counterpart of the male. Note that both the male and female are made in the image of God, and while biologically and transcendently (masculine and feminine) different, they are equal in dignity, value, and worth.

In Genesis 2:23–24, the related terms *ish* and *ishsha* are used for "man" and "woman." The man says, "She shall be called Woman [*ishsha*], because she was taken out of Man [*ish*]." English has different words for *woman* and *wife*. Not so, the Hebrew language of Proverbs. The same word, *ishshah*, is used for both. Determined by the context, the word means "woman, female, i.e. the biological female of a species in creation, counterpart of the male" or "wife, i.e. female spouse in a marriage union."[101]

Read

Read Proverbs 2:16-19; 6:23-26; 9:13; 11:22; 14:1.

What are the virtues practiced by a godly woman?

What are the vices practiced by an ungodly woman?

How should men relate to each type of woman?

Read Proverbs 31:10-31; 7:19-20; 21:9.

What are the virtues practiced by a godly wife?

What are the vices practiced by an ungodly wife?

How should a man act *virtuously* toward women and toward his wife?

If you are a woman, how might you reorder your life to be more godly, whether you are single or married?

If you are a man, how might you reorder your life to treat women with more dignity?

PARENTS AND CHILDREN

As we have seen earlier in the book (in chapter 4), the prologue of Proverbs (1:6–7) lists four purposes for the book:

- gaining wisdom and instruction
- understanding words of insight
- receiving instruction in prudent behavior
- giving prudence to those who are simple

Then comes a pivot. Wisdom is grounded in the fear of the Lord. How does this occur? By the education provided within the family by the mother and father:

Hear, my son, your father's instruction,
    and forsake not your mother's teaching,
for they are a graceful garland for your head
    and pendants for your neck. (Prov. 1:8–9)

Note, first of all, that the home is the cradle of education. The family, not the state, is responsible for the education of children; the family is the primary school for children. Note further that both parents are the instructors of their children. Parents are the adornment that grace the head and neck of their children.

God calls parents to teach their children His ways. He instructs children to keep the teachings of their parents. Thus, when children become parents, they can teach their own children. Families are the first platform in the creation for disseminating truth and building godly culture.

The Bible emphasizes that both parts of the equation work together. The father and mother enjoy teaching their sons and daughters;[102] the sons and daughters enjoy the company and teaching of their parents. The child is humble, quick to receive instruction from her parents. The children's understanding grows as they learn from their parents.

Both father and mother are teachers of their children (see Prov. 1:8). We see in chapter 31:1 that the future king is taught by his mother. The mother is a fount of knowledge, understanding, and wisdom; if she were not, she would not be in a position to instruct her offspring.

For good or ill, whether knowingly or not, children serve as ambassadors for their families to the world. Offspring can bring joy or shame to their parents. Humble, godly children love the law put in place by their parents. Proverbs affirms a norm for godliness: godly parents nurturing godly daughters and sons, resulting in a godly family.[103]

A father may not exercise the wisdom enjoined in Proverbs. A mother may use the language of the harlot portrayed in Proverbs. Perhaps they have not learned to control their anger, or to discipline their children appropriately. Perhaps the child is foolish and doesn't want to listen to his parents. Many young people take the attitude, "I don't need anyone's advice." We have all been influenced by bad company. These are examples of the failure to appropriate wisdom in the development of family life.

PRINCIPLES FOR FAMILY LIFE

Proverbs gives us principles to follow. We live in a day of pragmatism. People often want "Five Easy Steps to Successful Parenting." But the Bible knows nothing of such an approach. When truth is reduced to pragmatism, we have only the technique, the how. God is interested in humans understanding the what and the why. It is the biblical vision of the family and family life that answers the why and gives meaning to the what and the how.

As we have seen in our study of Wisdom, God created the universe to be holy and harmonious. He made human beings to live in unity and diversity within the human family and among families within communities. As the universe is a grand harmony, so was the intention of the family.

Author and columnist Janie B. Cheaney wrote a remarkable piece about the relationship between musical harmony and the harmony within the family. Her insights are powerful because what she says is born from the grand harmony and perfection of creation, being a product of the pan-harmony and perfection of the Creator.

> I've been researching various forms of creative expression for a possible book, and the branch of the arts that fascinates me most is the one I know least about: music. The main thing about music is relationship. Melody consists not in individual notes, but in the intervals between them. The ancient (and possibly mythical) philosopher Pythagoras discovered that dividing a lyre string in half produces an octave, while three-quarters of the string sounds a fourth and two-thirds sounds a perfect fifth. These mathematical ratios produce a pleasing musical progression known the world over. Based on this external framework, Western music established principles of harmony and melody that endured all the way up until the early twentieth century. And what happened then?
>
> Contemporary composer John Adams put it this way: "I learned in college that tonality died somewhere around the time that Nietzsche's God died, and I believed it." No God, no order. Musical structure collapsed, clearing the way for Arnold Schoenberg, who composed pieces built on abstract principles of numerology. From there it was only a step or two to John Cage, who tossed dice to pick the notes for his compositions and staged "symphonies" around

kitchen appliances. Not all avant-garde composers abandoned tonality, but music cut off from its defining structure ceased to be anything we would recognize as music.

Likewise, what defines society is relationships, built not on mathematical ratios but biology. It's an undeniable fact that, among humans, a male sperm joined to a female egg produces a human being.[104]

As Cheaney describes, a man and a woman are intended to form a family. The outcome of their love making is a child that enhances that family. This is the harmony of the smallest of human communities, launched, as Cheaney points out, at the nascent level, by two elements, one male and one female. But the child conceived in a one-night stand is deprived of a harmonious family and becomes embroiled in a series of dissonant relationships. Cheaney continues:

> The results of these random couplings drift like little wanderers from one family-like arrangement to another but never forge strong connections, except perhaps for a fraught relationship with Mom.
>
> Like music, community was once based on standard chords and intervals: the so-called nuclear family of father, mother, and child. Flexible enough for many variations, strong enough to sustain a melody. Without it, the hum of community lapses into noise.[105]

Proverbs gives parents principles for establishing a healthy and stable home where mother, father, and children can thrive. In Proverbs we see that parents should do the following:

- Submit to each other.[106] They need to stay open to correction from each other. They should also maintain humility as they lead their children.
- Keep company with godly people so as to provide the same for their children.
- Direct their children on the right path.
- Exercise self-discipline and not be afraid to discipline their children.
- Help their children develop life skills.
- Have control of the home.

Children also have a share in the development of a godly home. Children should do the following:·

- Honor their parents. This includes listening to their instruction and receiving their correction.
- Choose their friends wisely, surrounding themselves with godly people.
- Avoid bringing shame to their parents, but rather be a blessing in all they do.

Here's one overriding principle: both parents and children should love and revere God.

CHARACTERISTICS OF A GODLY HOME

What does a godly family look like? What is true of a godly home? Proverbs has much to say by way of answer to these important questions.

> ### Reflect
> Think of your own family life:
> As you were growing up, what were the *good* things in the life of your family?
> As you were growing up, what were the *painful* things in the life of your family?
> What are some of the characteristics of a godly family?

A godly home is marked by the following:

- Love for God and for one another.
- Respect for one another. Parents should demonstrate respect toward their children, and children must practice respect toward their parents.
- Disciplined living. Parents must cultivate the ability to receive discipline from God. They are responsible for the discipline of their children, who are expected to receive the same from their parents.
- Diligence of life. A godly family is not slothful or complacent about life. They exemplify hard work and the development of what God has entrusted to them.
- Parents passing on their faith to their children, showing the fear of God, providing structure and teaching morals.

- Both parents present physically, emotionally, and spiritually.
- Parents who affirm and guide their children. Constructive criticism and encouragement are key to a child's confidence.

Read

Read Proverbs 6:20-26; 22:6; 28:7; 10:1; 19:26-27; 20:7; 29:3; 30:17; 29:15.

What are the roles of the parents in a family and society?

What virtues are practiced by godly parents? What vices are practiced by ungodly parents?

What are the virtues of godly children? What are the vices practiced by ungodly children?

What has most impressed or challenged you in this study?

Write five principles to guide children to be godly and five principles to guide parents to be godly.

What could you have done to be a more godly parent or child?

What might you do now to make amends with your parents or children?

THE ELDERLY

A third dimension of family life addressed in Proverbs is the elderly. Proverbs calls us to use wisdom in our view and treatment of the elderly.

Read

Read Proverbs 3:1-2; 10:27; 13:3; 20:29; 9:10-11; 16:31; 22:4-6.

What tends to contribute to living a longer life? A shorter life?

How can our lifestyles contribute to a long life? An early death?

What are you doing now that will lend to your growing old and wise?

What can you do to show honor to the gray heads in your life? Be specific.

The global youth culture has one view of the elderly; the Bible has another. Some in the former regard elders as tiresome and irrelevant. Older people fade into the scenery, seldom honored or respected. Youth often fail to appreciate or listen to their elders. From the biblical point of view, long life is a reward for keeping the law of God. We should respect and honor our elders. Generally speaking, old age is accompanied by wisdom. The classroom of life has taught our elders many lessons. Those who have been wise have listened to the "gray headed" and have matured and profited from their wisdom.

Of course, old age is not tantamount to wisdom. The one who has foolishly disregarded life's lessons never becomes wise, but continues to live in immaturity even in old age. But those who have been wise reach prosperity and honor. Their years of experience bestow an appreciation for justice.

We need to bridge the gap between the generations. The elderly are a rich source of wisdom and blessing for the younger generation, if the latter will take time to build relationships with their grandparents and other elders.

Reflect

How are the elderly looked upon in your culture?

Today's world places enormous emphasis on youth culture. What impact does that have on how you see and relate to the older generation?

How would you describe the state of the family in your country?

Make a list of five things you will do, over your lifetime, to strengthen your family and families in your community.

14

Social Development

Friends and Neighbors

Genesis 11 records an intriguing story, the building of the tower of Babel.

> Now the whole earth had one language and the same words. And as people migrated from the east, they found a plain in the land of Shinar and settled there. And they said to one another, "Come, let us make bricks, and burn them thoroughly." And they had brick for stone, and bitumen for mortar. Then they said, "Come, let us build ourselves a city and a tower with its top in the heavens, and let us make a name for ourselves, lest we be dispersed over the face of the whole earth." And the LORD came down to see the city and the tower, which the children of man had built. And the LORD said, "Behold, they are one people, and they have all one language, and this is only the beginning of what they will do. And nothing that they propose to do will now be impossible for them. Come, let us go down and there confuse their language, so that they may not understand one another's speech." So the LORD dispersed them from there over the face of all the earth, and they left off building the city. Therefore its name was called Babel, because there the LORD confused the language of all the earth. And from there the LORD dispersed them over the face of all the earth. (Gen. 11:1–9)

God intended that mankind spread out over the earth. He had mandated the same: "Fill the earth and subdue it" (Gen. 1:28). "Be fruitful and multiply and fill the earth" (Gen. 9:1). He had founded the world and wanted man to cultivate and develop it. For that reason, He confused the languages at Babel and "dispersed" the people "over the face of the earth." But notice that He did not indict the builders at Babel. In fact, their sense of community and need to help one another was part of their nature as *imago Dei* creatures.

Just a few chapters earlier in Genesis we see another example of the importance of relationships. God punishes Cain, the first murderer, by making him "a fugitive and a wanderer on the earth" (Gen. 4:12). The first murderer becomes the first outcast, bereft of the wealth of relationships by which humans thrive. To this day, modern penal codes continue to use solitary confinement as an appropriate punishment.

In the Three-in-One God, community existed before the creation of the world. He is the One-and-the-Many God. Within the framework of the community that is Himself, God made us, His image bearers, for community also. He made us for relationships We need relationships. We can never fully know who we are without community, without connections to one another. In isolation we languish. We are closest to God's intentions for us when we are with others. This is true not only for our family, friends, and neighbors; it is true with those for whom we would not expect it to be true. When our lives intersect with the stranger and the poor, we become more of what God intends us to be. Anyone who befriends strangers, especially those who are poor or disenfranchised, becomes more human in the process.

Rabbi Daniel Lapin, in his book *Thou Shalt Prosper*, says, "Stay connected to others: you'll be happier and live longer."

> It is interesting that in his revelation to humanity, among his 10 pronouncements, rather than ask us to pray or bring sacrifices, or even take care of the poor, God focuses on a relationship-building program. By connecting with many other humans and maintaining those relationships, you will be able to increase your wealth, but that is not all. . . .
>
> Here's some evidence. According to a landmark study involving 222 cardiac patients and carried out by Nancy Fraser-Smith of the Montreal Heart Institute, patients who suffer heart attacks and are depressed are four times as likely to die in the following six months as those who are not depressed. . . .
>
> And the number one cause of depression? Dr. Gunnar Biorck examined 223 cardiac patients in the town of Malmo, Sweden, and

found that the most serious medical problems were encountered by these patients after they left hospital. He wrote that a special problem in convalescence is the lack of contact with friends, neighbors, and family. Under those conditions, feelings of loneliness and then depression present themselves. Health and human companionship do go hand in hand, says Dr. James Lynch in his book *The Broken Heart: The Medical Consequences of Loneliness.*[107]

Proverbs speaks of the importance of relationships, including relationships beyond the family. In this chapter we will consider the importance of relationships with friends and "neighbors" and the application of wisdom through the social virtues.

The book of Proverbs provides us with a series of couplets, virtues and vices that can govern our relationships in the larger community.

- love versus hate
- loyalty (faithfulness) versus disloyalty (unfaithfulness)
- kindness versus cruelty
- peace versus strife

As we live with virtue in our relationships—with family members, friends, neighbors, or strangers—an atmosphere of growth and flourishing occurs in our lives and theirs. If we relate to others with the contrary vice, personal destruction, degeneration, human conflict, and war will follow. Healthy relationships flow from a fount of wisdom. How important it is to consider our connections outside our immediate and extended family. Connections matter. It's important to develop these relationships because God wants us to enrich their lives and vice versa.

In his book *The Four Loves*, C. S. Lewis treats the quartet of loves as revealed in the language of the Greek New Testament. The first is *agape*, unconditional love. A second is *eros*, romantic love. *Storge* is the affection of the familiar (such as family). Finally, there is *phileo*, the love of friendship. His chapter on *phileo* includes an intriguing observation. Lewis was part of a close group of friends that enjoyed spending time together. He writes:

In each of my friends there is something that only some other friend can fully bring out. By myself I am not large enough to call the whole man into activity. I want other lights than my own to show all his facets. Now that Charles is dead, I shall never again see Ronald's reaction to a specifically Caroline joke. Far from having more of Ronald, having him "to myself" now that Charles is away, I have less of Ronald. Hence true Friendship is the least jealous of loves. Two friends delight to be joined by a third, and three by a fourth. . . . For in this love "to divide is not to take away."[108]

Reflect

List the various circles of relationships in your life beyond your immediate family.

Let's consider groups of people beyond extended family with whom we can foster relationships:

- near neighbors
- far neighbors (from other nations and cultures)
- friends at school
- friends at work
- friends at church
- other social networks
- strangers
- the poor
- enemies

Some of the groups will look familiar. Others, maybe not. We'll return to some of these categories below, but for now it is worth noting a couple things Jesus said on this subject.

"You have heard that it was said, 'You shall love your neighbor and hate your enemy.' But I say to you, Love your enemies and pray for those who persecute you.'" (Matt. 5:43–44)

"But when you give a feast, invite the poor, the crippled, the lame, the blind." (Luke 14:13)

Read

Read Proverbs 3:27–29; 25:8–10, 16–18, 21–22; 28:27; 29:5.

How are we to relate to the following?

Our neighbors

Strangers

Our enemies

The poor

Reflect

We normally think of the word *neighbor* in its noun form. The adjective form of the word is *neighborly*. The verb is *to neighbor*. How do you neighbor someone?

How does God want us to treat the poor? Why?

Why would God want us to love our enemies?

What does it look like to love our enemies?

Now let's examine the virtue of love and the vice of hate in human relations.

LOVE VERSUS HATE

Reflect

In your own words, what does it mean to love? To hate?

Give an example from your own experience of someone who loved someone who was unlovable.

Give an example from your own experience of seeing hate in the world.

Relationships are like fire: they can bring blessing or cause destruction. Each of us needs others in our life, but the trajectory of a relationship depends, in part, on the posture we take toward one another. For example, if we love others, we can be on the path to the kind of bonding that develops powerful relationships. But an insincere love or lukewarm affection cannot bear much fruit in a friendship.

The original language of Proverbs has a primary word for love, and for hate as well. The Hebrew word for love, *ahabah*, means "a state or condition of strong affection for another based on relationship. Note: this relationship can be familial, as a friend, properly romantic, or based in covenant." One thing to notice here is the tie between affection, or love, and relationship. When the Bible calls us to love our neighbor, that entails a relationship with that neighbor.

Read

Read Proverbs 10:12; 15:17; 17:9, 17; 26:24-26.

What are the characteristics of love? Of hate?

Reflect

Are there people you have hated that you need to forgive or love instead?

How might you love the unlovely better?

We all know what it's like to be loved by someone and to be hated by someone. We also know what it's like to love someone and to hate someone. As Proverbs 10:12 reminds us, "Hatred stirs up conflict, but love covers over all wrongs." In fact, hatred of a person is cancerous to one's own soul.

Love's triumph over hate is illustrated by the life of Louis Zamperini. I (Darrow) was first introduced to Zamperini by Laura Hillenbrand's remarkable biography *Unbroken: A World War II Story of Survival, Resilience, and Redemption*, the best book I read in the first decade of the new century.

Zamperini was an Olympian runner who later enlisted in the US Army Air Forces. His bomber crashed into the Pacific Ocean during World War II. Zamperini and a companion survived forty-seven days on a life raft before being picked up by the Japanese. Zamperini then spent two and a half years in a number of Japanese prisoner of war camps. In two of the camps, a sadistic camp commander, Mutsuhiro Watanabe, dubbed "the Bird" by the POWs, sought to break Zamperini with beatings, torture, and every kind of deprivation. At the end of the war, Watanabe was declared a war criminal because of his abuse of prisoners.

Hatred grew in Zamperini's heart for this man who so brutally abused him. His hatred was so great he wanted to kill him, even if it meant dying in the process. This part of Zamperini's life is the story of survival through the sheer strength of will.

In the second half of Louis Zamperini's story, he finds forgiveness through the love of Christ and redemption in the blood of Christ. God changed his cancerous heart of hatred to a heart of love. Zamperini found his life's calling in extending forgiveness to the Japanese people, especially those who ran the POW camps, places of inhumanity that had killed, maimed, and broken so many Allied prisoners. After his redemption, Louis traveled the world preaching love and its manifestation in forgiveness. He talked personally with former prison guards, extending love and forgiveness. Zamperini publicly forgave Watanabe and sought to meet with him to extend the hand of forgiveness. Watanabe, steeped in hatred, refused to admit guilt. In his view, he had treated POWs appropriately, as hated enemies. He refused to see Zamperini and receive his offered forgiveness. These two men represent the fulfillment of the proverb: "Hatred stirs up conflict, but love covers over all wrongs."

Now let's examine the virtue of loyalty and the vice of unfaithfulness in human relations.

LOYALTY (FAITHFULNESS) VERSUS DISLOYALTY (UNFAITHFULNESS)

Reflect

In your own words, what does it mean to be loyal?

In your own words, what does it mean to be disloyal?

Give an example from your own experience of someone who was loyal to a friend in a difficult situation.

The word *faithfulness* in our English Bible translates a Hebrew term (*emeth*) that means "faithfulness, reliability, trustworthiness, i.e. a state or condition of being dependable and loyal to a person or standard; the faithful, trustworthy one." We are reading here about God's character. He is the source of faithfulness. He is supremely worthy to be trusted. And He calls us to emulate this character seen ultimately in Him.

Our English dictionary throws further light on the term faithfulness: "Firm in adherence to the truth and to the duties of religion; firmly adhering to duty; of true fidelity; loyal; true to allegiance; as a faithful subject; constant in the performance of duties or services; as a faithful servant. Observant of compact, treaties, true to one's word." Once again, note how sadly our language has eroded: this early lexicographer of American language makes multiple connections to (Christian) religion.

We also get some light on the subject by considering the opposite, unfaithfulness, or the adjective form, unfaithful. The Hebrew (*bagad*) used in Proverbs means "to be unfaithful, be faithless, break faith, i.e. not trustworthy or reliable to a person or standard; commit adultery, be unfaithful, i.e. have sex with partner that is not one's married spouse; a spiritual unfaithfulness to other gods; betray, act treacherously, i.e. to be faithless to a principle, person or group."

Filling out the definition of the English word, Webster says, "Not observant of promises, vows, allegiance or duty; violating trust or confidence; treacherous; perfidious; as an unfaithful subject; an unfaithful husband or wife; an unfaithful servant."

My friend from Uruguay, Dr. Jose Gonzales, founder and president of Semilla, Inc., has spent a lifetime studying political culture in South America. He has observed that the difference in the North American experiment and that of South America can be summarized by one word, *covenant*. Gonzales argues that the political culture of North America was formed by the concept of covenant that moved from the Old Testament to the New Testament, through the Reformation in Europe to the Puritans who came to the shores of what became the USA. The men and women who came from southern Europe to settle South America lacked the biblical concept of covenant. This deficit of a covenant background had a negative impact on the concept of family and led to a lack of faithfulness to marriage vows. It also showed up in enterprise, a dearth in a sense of responsibility in keeping business contracts and taking promises seriously in governance.[109]

In his book, Dr. Gonzales explores why the notion of covenant is so essential for the flourishing of societies. "The biblical covenant is a solemn promise made by a personal God whereby He enters into personal, individual relationship with each of us by oath. God swears by Himself, as He is ultimately faithful, committing Himself to us, who commit ourselves to Him. This is the very essence of love, the irrevocable gift of oneself, and it comes with a promise, of His ineffable blessing, eternal salvation and covenant blessing in time."[110] The concept of covenant creates a connection of loyalty in human relationships, the keeping of promises in business and political culture. At one time here in the West, two people could look each other in the eye, make a pledge, and shake hands, confident that the pledge would be kept. Think of the reams of legal documents and inordinate number of lawyers required to keep a modern society functioning because of the lack of trust in personal, business, and civic relationships!

Read

Read Proverbs 3:3-4; 11:13; 13:17; 20:6; 25:13, 19.

What are the characteristics of a person who is loyal and dependable?

What are the characteristics of a person who is unfaithful or disloyal?

Reflect

How trustworthy are you in relationship to—
  Your friends
  Keeping promises or commitments
  Being transparent in business dealings or in school

Identify one area where you can work on being more trustworthy. What will you do?

Now let's examine the virtue of kindness and the vice of cruelty in human relations.

KINDNESS VERSUS CRUELTY

Reflect

In your own words, what does it mean to be kind?

In your own words, what does it mean to be cruel?

Give an example from your own experience of someone who is usually always kind.

The word *kindness* in our English Bible comes from the well-known Hebrew term *hesed*. This larger-than-life word means "loyal love, unfailing kindness, devotion, i.e. a love or affection that is steadfast based on a prior relationship." It is translated as loving-kindness, mercy, loyalty, and righteousness. As you can see, the word captures a broad spectrum of meaning that encompasses a wholistic view of our attitude toward others. What a powerful term God chose to depict this virtue![111]

Writing thousands of years later in the context of a new republic built on biblical principles, Webster defined kindness as "good will; benevolence; that temper or disposition which delights in contributing to the happiness of others, which is exercised cheerfully in gratifying their wishes, supplying their wants or alleviating their distresses." The godly person takes the initiative and looks for opportunity to show kindness. Consider the example of King David, who asked, "Is there still anyone left of the house of Saul, that I may show him kindness for Jonathan's sake?" (2 Sam. 9:1). Kindness delights to give help where help is needed.

One opposite of kindness is cruelty. The adjective form is captured in Proverbs by a Hebrew term (*akzari*) meaning "cruel, merciless, i.e., pertaining to ruthless behavior toward another." Referencing Webster's 1828 dictionary we see his definition: "Disposed to give pain to others, in body or mind; willing or pleased to torment, vex or afflict; inhuman; destitute of pity, compassion or kindness; fierce; ferocious; savage; barbarous; hardhearted." Such a description applies to the great enemy of God; all who practice cruelty imitate the devil himself.

Read

Proverbs 11:16-17; 12:25; 14:22; 19:22; 20:28; 31:26.
What are the characteristics of kindness? Of cruelty?

Reflect

How might you do an act of kindness in the next two days for the following people?
- A friend
- A stranger
- Someone with whom you have tension

We all have personal stories of cruelty and kindness we have received from or extended toward others. We also know of human cruelty and kindness of almost epic proportion. Hitler, Stalin, and Mao are examples of the former; William Wilberforce, Mother Teresa, and Pope John Paul II of the latter.

One such story is the life of John Merrick, portrayed in the 1980 film *The Elephant Man*. Merrick was born with a rare disorder known as Proteus syndrome that left him hideously deformed. The reaction of society to his appearance was the epitome of cruelty and bullying. Merrick was enslaved by his ruthless "owner," Mr. Bytes. Bytes put John on public exhibition in a Victorian London freak show. John was cruelly treated by society as a hideous and dumb animal.

Merrick was shown kindness by a London hospital surgeon, Dr. Frederick Treves. Treves provided Merrick a home, a room in the hospital where Treves worked. In response to this gift of mercy and kindness, Merrick revealed to Dr. Treves that he was not mute. Not only could he speak; he was quite bright. He had committed portions of the Bible to memory and had a gift for the arts.

Cruelty destroys individual lives and communities. Kindness can bring healing and human flourishing even in the most broken people and communities. Mr. Bytes's cruelty to John Merrick deprived the world of knowing a truly remarkable man. Dr. Treves's act of kindness profoundly changed Merrick's life and the lives of all those who knew him. Despite his jarring external appearance, here was an *imago Dei* human.

Now let's examine the virtue of living peacefully and the vice of causing strife in human relations.

PEACE VERSUS STRIFE

Our final set of words in this chapter capture the idea of contributing toward a peaceful society versus bringing strife. The Hebrew term from which our English Bible translate "peace" is *shalom*, one of the most well-known Hebrew words among non-Hebrew speakers. It means "peace, prosperity, i.e. an intact state of favorable circumstance; completeness, i.e. the state of a totality of a collection; safeness, salvation, i.e. a state of being free from danger; health, i.e. a state of lack of disease and a wholeness or well-being; satisfaction, contentment, i.e. the state of having one's basic needs or more being met and so being content." Note again, in a fashion similar to *hesed*, the full-orbed nature of this word, and of its impact in a community or nation.

Our English word *peace*, according to Webster, means "in a general sense, a state of quiet or tranquility; freedom from disturbance or agitation; applicable to society, to individuals, or to the temper of the mind."

The contrasting Hebrew word, *madon*, means "strife, dissension, i.e. a verbal quarrel; source or object of contention." Here we have a "leaner" definition for a word rooted in vice, in the ugliness of anti-godly thinking. Webster, likewise, elaborates on the word *strife* thus: "Contention in anger or enmity; contest; struggle for victory; quarrel or war."

Read

Read Proverbs 12:20; 15:18; 16:28-29; 26:20-21; 28:25; 29:22.

What are the characteristic of a person who is peaceful?

What are the characteristic of a person who brings strife?

Reflect

Examine your own life. What are areas where you tend to create (maybe even enjoy creating) strife?

What are some practical ways you can be a peacemaker?

Reflect

We have been studying the virtues that help strengthen the community and social fabric of society and the vices that work to fray society.

List two or three things you are taking away from this session.

Develop a creative reflection in response to what you have learned about the necessity for social development. This might be a song, a poem, a monologue, a play with a group of others, or a prayer.

The Aramaic expression "the son of peace" refers to a person in a community or nation who seeks peace. This is a person of influence, often one who has a good reputation and provides an entry point for others to engage the larger community. When Jesus sent out His disciples two by two, He instructed them to identify the man of peace in the community (Luke 10:6) and engage with that person.

In the midst of the global conflict with radical Islamists, is there a man of peace? The world is waiting for that person. In a part of the world aflame with violence between Muslim communities (e.g., between Shia and Sunni), and Muslim violence toward Jews, secularists, Hindus, Buddhists, animists, and Christians, is there a man of peace?

Recently a man of stature in Egypt, the heart of the Islamic civilization, has spoken words of peace. That man is Egyptian President Abdel Fattah al-Sisi. On New Year's Day, 2015, at Al-Azhar University in Cairo, considered the leading center for Islamic studies in the world, Sisi spoke to a group of religious scholars celebrating the birthday of the prophet Mohammed. His words were a rousing call for the reformation of Islam. To his audience of Islamic scholars and religious leaders he asked the startling question:

> Is it possible that 1.6 billion people (Muslims worldwide) should want to kill the rest of the world's population—that is, 7 billion people—so that they themselves may live? . . . Impossible.
>
> You imams (prayer leaders) are responsible before Allah. The entire world—I say it again, the entire world—is waiting for your next move because this umma [a word that can refer either to the Egyptian nation or the entire Muslim world] is being torn, it is being destroyed, it is being lost—and it is being lost by our own hands.
>
> The corpus of texts and ideas that we have made sacred over the years, to the point that departing from them has become almost impossible, is antagonizing the entire world. You cannot feel it if you remain trapped within this mindset. You must step outside yourselves and reflect on it from a more enlightened perspective.
>
> We have to think hard about what we are facing. . . . It's inconceivable that the thinking that we hold most sacred should cause the entire Islamic world to be a source of anxiety, danger, killing, and destruction for the rest of the world. Impossible.[112]

President Sisi boldly called for peace to replace strife at the heart of the Muslim world. A week later the Coptic church was celebrating the Eastern observation of Christmas, and Sisi made a surprise visit to St. Mark's Coptic

Cathedral, the seat of the Coptic Orthodox Church and its Pope Tawadros II. He came bringing greetings during the Christmas Eve Mass. This was an unprecedented act in modern history. Sisi, himself a Muslim, risked death by Islamists to extend a hand of peace. May his actions and clarion call mark a turning point in Islam's relationship with the world!

Peace leads to human and national flourishing. Strife brings conflict and war, the destruction of human life, and the brokenness of communities and nations.

Each of the virtues we have studied—love, faithfulness, kindness, and peacefulness—is a manifestation of God's very nature. These virtues may be studied separately, but they are never to be separated. Springing from the heart of God, each virtue helps to define the others. As we live out these virtues, we witness, and encourage, human flourishing.

The corresponding vices—hatred, disloyalty, cruelty, and strife—are born from the heart of darkness. They infect our lives with a cancer that eats away at human relationships and communities. May God grant us the hearts to live the virtues in the midst of our human relationships.

15

Political Development

Some years ago I (Darrow) attended a lecture at Arizona State University. The presenting professor was an astronomer. Near the beginning of the lecture he mentioned that a majority of the people signing up for his class thought they were going to learn astrology!

Whether you find this story amusing or astounding, the student confusion reflects a shift from a biblical worldview to a postmodern one. Astronomy and astrology are very different. Both have to do with studying the heavens, but they are more like antonyms than synonyms.

Astronomy is a scientific discipline. It demonstrates that the planets—the sun, moon, and stars—help us govern our world. Astrology is an animistic system of magic that claims we are governed by the stars. Astronomy affirms that we are free moral human beings with the ability to rule the world God has made; to analyze, act creatively, and make real, moral decisions. Astrology makes us subjects of the fates. Our life is dictated by the stars. We are not free, but automatons, robots following a predetermined path.

On the fourth day of creation, God formed the heavenly bodies to "be lights in the expanse of the heavens to separate the day from the night, and let them be for signs and for seasons and for days and years" (Gen. 1:14 NASB). The sun, moon, and stars allow us to govern space and time. We govern time by establishing calendars marked by the orbit of the earth around the sun (one year), the orbit of the moon around the earth (one month), and the revolution of the earth on its axis (one day). We observe the sun, moon, and stars, and orient ourselves in space by creating maps of the sky and marking physical distances in our world.

On the sixth day, God created His image bearers—male and female—to govern the earth: "Then God said, 'Let us make man in our image, after our

189

likeness. And let them have dominion over the fish of the sea and over the birds of the heavens and over the livestock and over all the earth and over every creeping thing that creeps on the earth'" (Gen. 1:26). Human beings were made to govern the earth, to rule within (and by) the laws and ordinances of creation. These "fixed principles" are built into the universe. They comprise the framework for governing the creation as well as our own lives and the life of the larger community.

We were made to govern all of life, our own lives as well as the civil society we live in. Wisdom relates to all of life: business, family, governance, health care, education, child rearing, the arts, science, and so on. Wisdom thus provides for the enrichment of each person, family, and community.

As we have seen in Proverbs 3:13–15 and 8:10–11, wisdom is more important than silver and gold, more precious than rubies. Human beings are responsible, under the sovereign rule of their Creator, for the future of their lives, their families, their communities, and the building of their nations. Wisdom is the key to governing that leads to flourishing.

Reflect

Are all governments equal in the value they bring to a society? Why or why not?

What are the characteristics of a good government?

What are the characteristics of a bad government?

This chapter will consider three dimensions of how Proverbs informs political development. First, we will explore the nature of leadership. What is leadership, according to Proverbs? How does virtuous leadership present itself? What does bad leadership look like?

Second, we will think together about the necessity of justice. The administration of justice is one of the most important responsibilities of human leaders. The history of the nations has included unbridled corruption as well as examples of just and compassionate governing. We will seek the wisdom of Proverbs about justice.

The third aspect of political development we'll examine is the importance of planning. Societies marked by careful planning have been commensurately blessed. But some nations have never seen the benefits of planning—that is, the careful shaping of one's priorities and activities for the improvement of life for all. So this is also an important part of what we learn from Proverbs.

THE NATURE OF LEADERSHIP

Reflect

Identify someone you know who is a good leader. What makes him/ her a good leader?

How can failing leaders become good leaders?

God gave humans intellect and we are responsible to nurture and use it. A developed intellect enhances human endeavor, including leadership. Having said that, leadership and intelligence are not the same. Someone may be very smart but lack the wisdom necessary to exercise leadership.

Neither is true leadership a matter of inheritance or birth. A person may be born into a family of nobility, but nobility and leadership are different assets.

Read

Read Proverbs 8:14-16; 20:26-28; 25:15; 28:15-16; 29:2, 4; 29:12; 31:1-5.

List the characteristics of the following:
  • a godly leader
  • an ungodly leader

Where do you see each manifested today?

Leadership is based on character. Webster's defines character as "a mark made by cutting or engraving." What does this definition contribute to our understanding of leadership? Just this: God's image has been stamped onto every person. We are made in the image of God. This echo of God's nature is intrinsic to every human being. Because of this, our lives have significance and meaning. Effective leadership is the product of a godly life. Leadership is more about living a virtuous life than about simply being smart. Hosea

2:19–20 reveals the nature of God and thus the character of godly leaders: "I will betroth you to me forever; I will betroth you in righteousness and justice, in love and compassion. I will betroth you in faithfulness, and you will acknowledge the LORD."

From this text we see that the marks of a good leader include righteousness, justice, love, compassion, and faithfulness. When you compare these qualities with much of what is affirmed as leadership in today's world, you see a gap. To a considerable extent, we have a leadership deficit in the modern world because we educate for knowledge but not for virtue. We provide students—future leaders—with information but not with understanding and wisdom. In his book *The Abolition of Man*, C. S. Lewis put it like this: "We make men without chests and expect from them virtue and enterprise. We laugh at honor and are shocked to find traitors in our midst."[113] Lewis's words effectively describe the common condition of education and leadership in the West and Europe in the early years of the twenty-first century.

SERVANT LEADERSHIP

Let's consider two aspects of leadership rooted in godly character as we see it in Proverbs, beginning with servant leadership.

Government is ordained of God (see Rom. 13). In God's view, governments exist to serve the people. Because of the inherent corrupting nature of authority, governments too often come to believe that the people exist to serve the government. Proverbs 17:23 says, "The wicked accept bribes in secret to pervert the course of justice." Note the contrast between accepting bribes (a selfish corruption of authority) and guarding the course of justice (the exercise of authority to serve the people). Proverbs 15:27 takes a similar view: "The greedy bring ruin to their households, but the one who hates bribes will live."

The concept of public service to describe political leadership was first used in 1570. The British office of prime minister captures this view. "Minister" derives from the Latin *ministrare*, "to serve, attend, wait upon." Thus the prime minister is the "first servant." From 1620 the term was used as "first servant to the crown."[114]

Too often government service becomes a stepping stone to power and riches. This is backwards; the government exists for public service, not for the individual benefit of rulers. When those who govern serve themselves, when they use their authority to amass power, money, and influence, they corrupt themselves and their office. Sadly, many countries and communities remain underdeveloped because they have been impoverished by dictatorial control. This distortion of true leadership serves its own purposes and crushes the ambition of the citizen. Instead of encouraging the natural innovation of the people, dictatorial authority stifles such initiative. Successful entrepreneurs are stripped of the fruits of their labor through corruption, theft, and high taxes.[115] In contrast, servant leadership encourages the uniqueness of individual citizens and creates a vibrant arena of freedom to try new ideas.

Servant leadership encourages political and economic freedom. When individuals are free to flourish, communities and nations may flourish.

DELEGATED LEADERSHIP

A second aspect of godly leadership is the delegation of authority. But before there can be delegation, there must be someone with vision.

The King James Version of Proverbs 29:18 reads, "Where there is no *vision*, the people perish: but he that keepeth the law, happy is he." The Hebrew word for vision is *chazon*, meaning "to foresee or perceive." People need vision or foresight to see God's order and anticipate His coming kingdom. This is especially true among leaders. One ingredient of leadership is the ability to see ahead, to understand the times. Without this vision the nation will perish. To put it differently, visionary leadership is an important part of the flourishing of a nation.

In Exodus 18:13–27 we find the principle of delegated leadership. After the Hebrew people are brought out of slavery in Egypt and living as enslaved people for 430 years, they were operating from a slave mentality. Now God, through Moses, had set them free from slavery. But the slavery remained in their minds and it had to be removed. They were used to the dictatorial rule of Pharaoh. But Moses had a servant mentality (vv. 13–14). He was working hard on behalf of the people night and day, helping them solve their problems.

The account shows a progression of the principle of delegated authority.

1. Moses was overwhelmed by trying to serve the people by himself. Today we would say he was on the verge of burnout. Furthermore, the people were also weary (vv. 15–18).

2. Moses's father-in-law became the "prime minister" to Moses and gave him godly counsel.
3. Moses's leadership took on two primary functions. On the one hand, he was to bring the people's needs before God (v. 19). He served the people as a priest, representing them to God. On the other hand, he was to set God's laws and words before the people (v. 20). That is, he served as a prophet, representing God to the people, so that the people would know how to live and work ("show them the way to live and the duties they are to perform"). Godly leadership, manifested through a prophetic and priestly voice, was essential for the development of the nation.

These verses describe God's actions to transform a slave people with a slave mindset into a free people with a free mindset. He wanted His people to be lifted out of poverty and brought into human flourishing. But to flourish they needed to know how to live and how to work.

This divine purpose called for Moses to function from his gifting and let others function from theirs. Moses was to delegate authority, not to amass power to himself. He was to do this by selecting qualified individuals from among the people (v. 21a). The qualifications are spelled out as *able men* who *fear God*, men of *truth* who *hate covetousness*. These men were to be given delegated authority (vv. 21b–22) to equip them to judge in a manner appropriate to the gravity of the situation. Only the most serious issues would be brought to Moses. The delegated leaders would carry a load of responsibility and thus decrease Moses's load. The people's interests would be served in a timely and efficient manner.

As verse 23 indicates, if Moses does this, he will be able to handle his leadership responsibilities without collapsing under the load. And the people will have their disputes adjudicated. They will be able to live in peace.

THE NATURE OF LEADERSHIP: A SUMMARY

Proverbs shows us that biblical leadership includes integrity of thought and speech, servanthood, and careful insight. Godly leaders eschew cruelty and care for the marginalized. They guard their hearts against the selfish abuse of power. Rulers have greater responsibility to live in virtue because their choices affect many people (Prov. 31:1–5). They should not speak carelessly, but should guard their words since their influence can extend far and wide

(Prov. 16:10). Rulers are to be approachable. This calls for patience and gentle servanthood because the natural tendency is to protect oneself from intrusion (e.g., King Ahasuerus in Esther 4:11), but a leader cannot freely exercise this privilege; his people depend on their access to him. King David relinquished his right to grieve the death of his son in order to show appreciation for the army that had put down Absalom's rebellion (2 Sam. 18:24–19:8).

THE NECESSITY OF JUSTICE

Prepare

Describe in your own words the concept of justice.

Describe in your own words the concept of corruption.

How does corruption or injustice affect a city? A nation?

A second dimension of political development is the necessity of justice. An intimate relationship exists between doing justice and achieving happiness. We see this in Proverbs 29:18b (KJV), "He that keepeth the law, happy is he."

The British jurist Sir William Blackstone was one of the great legal scholars of the eighteenth century. In a remarkable and eloquent statement he captured this link between justice and happiness: "For He [God] has so intimately connected, so inseparably interwoven the laws of eternal justice with the happiness of each individual, that the latter cannot be attained but by observing the former; and, if the former be punctually obeyed, it cannot but induce the latter."[116]

In the modern world, we tend to equate happiness with license, that is, freedom from moral constraint. A life of license is deemed the ultimate route to happiness. But wisdom shows that happiness is found when we pursue justice. We live in a world ordered by God. We were designed to live within that order. And as we pursue justice, we will find happiness. To live a life of license is to find only misery. Consider King Solomon, for example. Ironically, the same individual who wrote so many proverbs early in his life came to emptiness and futility after indulging every license imaginable. In our day, we think of celebrities like Michael Jackson or Marilyn Monroe, individuals who had everything, yet apparently found little meaning in life. The *Wall Street Journal* recently reported that "a new study co-funded by the Gates Foundation . . . portrays the ultra-rich as lost souls burdened by the fears, worries and family distortions of too much money."[117] Think of Kurt Cobain, the Nirvana rock star of global fame who took his own life at twenty-seven years of age. Or think of Robin Williams, the number-one comedian and one of the great movie stars of all times. And one of the most beautiful and famous actresses, Marilyn Monroe, took her own life. Many people who have achieved wealth and fame find only emptiness.

The conduct of a nation is reflected in the collective moral conscience of her people. Proverbs 14:34 declares, "Righteousness exalts a nation, but sin condemns any people." In other words, a nation's greatness is found in its moral character. Does the nation promote justice for all her people? If so, she will be exalted on the international stage. But a nation where slavish behavior and injustice prevails will be condemned to poverty and servitude.

Reflect

Are all governments established by righteousness (Prov. 16:12)?

Identify a government (or the characteristics of a government) that is not righteous.

Should people living in a country ruled by tyranny obey or disobey the tyrant? Why or why not?

Inherent in this matter of justice is the standard by which judgment is rendered. Only that external standard found in God's character and manifested in the moral law provides the foundation for true justice. God's creation laws establish an objective standard. Attempts to impose a "justice" based on subjective standards, whether a cultural fad or a tyrant's fancy, cannot succeed. Only those principles grounded in the Creator's purposes comprise a worthy pattern by which laws can be made and judgments carried out.

Justice lies on the opposite end of the spectrum from corruption. In the same way that a just culture reflects the character of God, a corrupt culture mirrors the cult—the worship—of pagan deities who can be bribed. Cultures that revere idols, corruptions of the one true God, become corrupt themselves. The psalmist said, speaking of idols, "Those who make them will be like them, and so will all who trust in them" (Ps. 115:4–8).

But Scripture is clear: the God of the universe is just and rules in justice. "For the LORD your God is God of gods and Lord of lords, the great God, mighty and awesome, who shows no partiality and accepts no bribes" (Deut. 10:17).

Read

Read Proverbs 12:17; 17:15; 19:28; 21:3, 15; 24:23-26; 28:4-9.

What do these passages reveal about truthful and false witnesses?

What do they reveal about the just and the corrupt?

When it comes to justice, the living God shows no partiality and calls His people to the same (Prov. 24:23; 28:21). The blindfold on Lady Justice as depicted in the public squares of many nations represents God's impartiality. His righteous judgment is not influenced by an individual's age, wealth, sex, size, color of skin, and so on. Nor can He be bribed.

Likewise, the earthly magistrate is to judge justly, neither punishing the innocent for lack of a bribe or setting a guilty man free because of a bribe. If imposing a fine on the innocent is not good, surely to flog honest officials is not right (Prov. 17:26).

Reflect

How does a culture of trust affect a nation?

How does a culture of distrust affect a nation?

What are some areas in your life where you could be more transparent?

A people is not to be judged by a subjective, internal standard that can be changed at the whim of the magistrate.

THE IMPORTANCE OF PLANNING

Finally, let's consider one more dimension of political development, the importance of planning.

> **Reflect**
>
> What is a plan?
>
> What does planning look like in your culture?
>
> Why is planning important?
>
> What is the opposite of planning?
>
> Why is it important for an individual or a government to plan?

Many cultures do not have a framework for planning. They may be trapped in some kind of fatalistic mindset: "We can't change the future, so why plan? It's better to take things as they come and deal with them as best you can." Other cultures don't recognize the reality of the future at all. For them, there is only the past or present. There is no sense of progress. There is only this moment and the past to return to. The present is one endless continuum where one day is the same as another. In such societies there is no concept of future.

Fatalism has locked many *imago Dei* humans into a cycle of helplessness, dependency, and futility. A fatalist mindset says, "We are ruled by the stars. My destiny is already written and there is nothing I can do about it. We were born poor, we will die poor. Life is a circle, it simply repeats itself." We see this even in some popular movies that speak of "the great circle of life." "It is written"[118] or "History is something that happens to me" are the mantras of fatalism.

This contrasts with the Judeo-Christian mindset on which the West was founded. This worldview recognizes that history is real, and that history is going somewhere. A grand, divine purpose permeates human existence. All things were created with intentionality. There is a great end toward which history is moving.

God's creative purpose includes a powerful truth: a human being is a free moral agent, responsible to help shape the future. Humans are free. We are not victims of a hostile cosmos. We are not governed by the stars (the lie of astrology); rather, the stars are given to help us to govern our lives and order our world (the truth of astronomy). The future can be different; things can be better than they are today.

The Bible portrays a reality that includes progress toward the fruition of all things, the cosmic redemption in which all things will be made new. This includes progress in the material realm, in the aesthetic realm, and in the realm of knowledge and understanding. The cry of a free people is not "history is something that happens to me" but "history is something I make!" When we think with a biblical mind, we are able to see God's hand at work and the place He has for us. Because of the biblical mind, we can plan for the future.

We live in a reality that allows us to change, to grow, to improve our lives. We are not locked in a cage; we are free. We can move from point A to point B. Our families do not need to stay in poverty. Our communities may progress toward God's good intentions. We can build nations that are free and not enslaved, compassionate and not cruel, prosperous and not poor, just and not corrupt.

We wrote earlier about God's gift of the heavenly bodies that allow us to govern in space and time. We travel beyond the earth's atmosphere into space, first in our dreams and imaginations, then in actual time and space. We have sent astronauts to the moon. We have deployed space vehicles to land on Mars and to journey beyond our solar system.

In the meantime, we apply divinely enabled planning abilities *on* our planet as well. We create roads and bridges that allow us to move from one place to another. We create technologies to explore mountains and rivers, even the depth of the oceans. We have probed inner space as well, the realm of the atoms and subatomic particles. The Human Genome Project has mapped our DNA and the human genetic code, making new medical advances possible.

God's design of the creation has enabled humans to govern time. We have created clocks and calendars by which we mark seconds, minutes, hours, days, weeks, years, decades, centuries, and millennia. Given their familiarity, these concepts can seem mundane, but they have allowed for the recording of history! We can distinguish not only day and night but also past, present, and future. It's almost impossible to imagine human life without these concepts and distinctions that are so fundamental to our learning, growth, and flourishing.

In fact, human beings are partners with the sovereign God of the universe in the shaping of history, in creating the future. As we finish this chapter, let's consider three applications that derive from that truth.

Read

Read Proverbs 4:26; 14:15; 15:22; 16:3, 9; 21:5, 29-31; 22:3, 5.

What is the nature of planning?

How does the providence of God intersect with our planning?

List other insights on planning and its opposite, carelessness.

First, although humans are partners with God in shaping the future, we do not share in His perfections. We are in fact fallen. So when we are making plans, it is important to hear multiple opinions. We read, for example, in Proverbs 11:14, "For lack of guidance a nation falls, but victory is won through many advisers." Again, in 15:22, "Plans fail for lack of counsel, but with many advisers they succeed." Given the limitations of our finiteness and propensity to sin, when we make plans it is wise to consult many counselors: family, friends, mentors, and leaders. These can both give us godly counsel and hold us accountable.

Second, good planning requires time and careful effort. Proverbs 21:5 (NLT) says, "Good planning and hard work lead to prosperity, but hasty shortcuts lead to poverty." Planning requires self-discipline, the application of restraint, and delayed gratification. People who are ruled by their emotions make foolish decisions that lead to poverty. We need to take time to plan well, to examine alternatives, and to assess whether our plans will achieve our goals or lead to unintended consequences. The old saying "Haste makes waste!" captures the truth of the need to take care in planning.

Waiting for the lottery to make you rich will only lead to poverty. Waiting for someone who is wealthy to give you money will build dependency and poverty of life and spirit. Planning and hard work are virtues that lead to human flourishing. "The wisdom of the prudent is to give thought to their ways, but the folly of fools is deception" (Prov. 14:8).

Reflect

Place yourself on the following scale:

A planner <----------------------> *Impulsive*

For a nation to be free, its citizens need to be internally self-governing. What does this mean?

What is required to maintain order in a society as citizens become increasingly lawless?

What are the most significant things you have learned about political development?

List what you have learned about principles of governance.

Finally, we need to think about where we are going and how we will get there. Without goals, we wander aimlessly through life. If you have a goal, you can make plans on how to get there from today. Our best-laid plans connect to God's purposes in history.

Proverbs 16:3 says, "Commit to the LORD whatever you do, and he will establish your plans." Each person has been made unique for a purpose. God gives each person the opportunity to connect their life with His larger purposes for creation. God wants to connect our story to His story for the making of history. When we understand our calling, we can order our life and work toward that calling. We can seek the education, skills, and certification that will allow us to do what we have been made to do.

As we acknowledge and live out God's wise governance in our homes, communities, and nations, we will flourish.

16

Economic Development

Prepare

Make a list of the principles or virtues you have learned from your reading that contribute to economic development.

Make a list of the vices you have discovered that would contribute to economic poverty.

Culture is a universal phenomenon; to live together in human community is to experience culture. Cultures have legitimate differences. For example, one culture may emphasize the nuclear family, while another culture places more value on extended family. But these differences should not disguise an important reality: not all cultures have equally positive effects on a society.

For example, cultures have different levels of positive contribution to economic development. Here are cultural traits that build robust economies:

- strong families
- commitment to the larger community
- compassion toward fellow human beings
- concern for educational application of knowledge, understanding, and wisdom
- moral leadership
- awareness of evil and willingness to fight against it
- justice in society
- generosity
- honesty and integrity
- freedom and responsibility

Maybe the most important cultural trait for economic development is a strong work ethic. Proverbs offers an interesting model for a good work ethic.

LOOK AT THE ANT

Proverbs 6:6–11 is one of the classic passages on economic health. The writer points to the lowly ant as a model for hard work and individual responsibility.

> Go to the ant, you sluggard;
>> consider its ways and be wise!
>
> It has no commander,
>> no overseer or ruler,
>
> yet it stores its provisions in summer
>> and gathers its food at harvest.
>
> How long will you lie there, you sluggard?
>> When will you get up from your sleep?
>
> A little sleep, a little slumber,
>> a little folding of the hands to rest—
>
> and poverty will come on you like a thief
>> and scarcity like an armed man. (NIV)

Read

Read and discuss Proverbs 6:6-11.

List the virtues and vices related to economic health.

In this final chapter we will consider economic development—well-being, wealth, and poverty in human communities. We'll discuss four virtues of wealth creation: conservation, industriousness, thrift, and generosity.

God's intentions for human life include economic health, not poverty. God designed the creation for human flourishing, a comprehensive framework that incorporates economic dimension. That is not to affirm the popular "health and wealth" teaching. For one thing, the Bible does not teach that Christ followers deserve to be rich and free from trouble. God often allows suffering in the life of the believer for purposes of developing character, for example. Beyond that, too often the underlying theme of the "health and wealth" doctrine is personal consumption.

The Bible generally speaks of wealth as a blessing and poverty as a curse. Poverty (which transcends financial hardship) divides people. It alienates and isolates humans. It robs people of hope, and mocks their dignity as *imago Dei* creatures. The impoverished are dependent. They lack what is normal in society.

Peter Greer, president and CEO of HOPE International, wrote an article at the Institute for Faith, Work & Economics titled "How People Who Live on Less than Two Dollars a Day Taught Me to Redefine Poverty."[119] HOPE International interviewed twenty people, most of whom lived on less than two dollars per day, and asked them how they define poverty. According to these people, poverty is the following:

- an empty heart
- not knowing your abilities and strengths
- not being able to make progress
- isolation
- no hope or belief in yourself, knowing you can't take care of your family
- broken relationships
- not knowing God
- not having basic things to eat
- not having money
- a consequence of not sharing
- a lack of good thoughts

Wealth, on the other hand, builds community. Proverbs 19:4 says wealth "makes many friends." True wealth is related to righteousness. Wealth opens many avenues to blessing others, creating ways to disciple the nations.

NEITHER POVERTY NOR RICHES

From the perspective of the Bible, both poverty and riches include potential hazards for the person wishing to live in virtue. Consider a classic passage on economic health:

Two things I ask of you;
    deny them not to me before I die:

Remove far from me falsehood and lying;
> give me neither poverty nor riches;
> feed me with the food that is needful for me,
lest I be full and deny you
> and say, "Who is the LORD?"
or lest I be poor and steal
> and profane the name of my God. (Prov. 30:7–9)

Read

Read and discuss Proverbs 30:7-9.

List the virtues and vices related to economic health.

The Hebrew word translated "wealth" (*hon*), in its verb form, means "to own possessions desirable in a society, *enough*, i.e. *what is sufficient.*" Webster's 1828 further elaborates on the term *wealth*: "Prosperity; external happiness. Riches; large possessions of money, goods or land; that abundance of worldly estate which exceeds the estate of the greater part of the community; *affluence; opulence.*"

The Hebrew concept of poverty (*resh*), in like fashion, denotes "*poverty, i.e. a state or condition of lacking what is needed,* below what is normal in society." From Webster's we get "destitution of property; indigence; want of convenient means of subsistence. The consequence of poverty is dependence."

Note that the Hebrew and English definitions of poverty are similar, but the definitions of wealth are different.

Let's see how Proverbs views wealth and poverty.

Read

Read Proverbs 3:9-10, 13-16; 11:4, 24-28; 17:16; 22:1-2, 4; 23:4-5; 28:19-20.

What do these passages reveal about wealth and poverty?

What are the restrictions on gaining material wealth?

What wealth is greater than material wealth?

How is material wealth a blessing? A hindrance?

CONSERVATION

As mentioned previously, wealth creation requires four virtues. Let's begin with conservation.

We noted Proverbs' praise of the ant, which "stores its provisions in summer and gathers its food at harvest." Here is an example built by God at the creation, a lowly creature that models for humans the importance of saving in preparation for an emergency.

A group of students recently made the following observations about the virtue of conservation:

- We need to be good administrators of what we have.
- The wise know how to administer their goods and keep them like a treasure. The foolish just consume and waste them.
- God gave us planet earth. We have not been good conservers and now we face consequences; our planet has been warning us and we don't care.
- Because we don't conserve, we end up in debt. We think only of the present: "If I like it, I'll buy it." Then an emergency comes and we have no money. Think long-term. Think of your grandchildren. Save to leave them an inheritance, not debt.
- The church is preaching a message (the prosperity gospel) that leads to poverty.

> ### Read
> Read Proverbs 12:10; 21:20; 27:23-27; 28:19.
>
> What do these verses reveal about our care for creation?
>
> What best describes your own habits: a consumer of creation, a conserver of creation, or a worshiper of creation (some would say "environmentalist")?

INDUSTRIOUS VERSUS LAZY

A second virtue necessary for economic well-being is industry (or its adjective form, industrious). A helpful synonym is *diligence*. Generally speaking, the diligent or industrious person prospers. The opposite is also true: the lazy person will always be in need. The slothful person will live in failure and misery. "Slothfulness casts into a deep sleep, and an idle person will suffer hunger" (Prov. 19:15).

Contrary to the opinion of many people, work is not punishment. Rather, work is God's gift to humans. It is one way we worship and glorify our Creator. In fact, the Hebrew word (*abodah*) means both work and worship. In much of the world, work and worship are separated: worship is a spiritual activity, and work is resigned to a worldly activity. But in the integrated mind of the Hebrew people this is not the case. Work is an act of worship. We do our work as unto the Lord. This is a radical concept for most societies today.

An industrious nation and its people can be free and live without being dependent on others. To bless the nation, we need to work.

Work is a biblical virtue. That means that if a nation is going to benefit from this virtue, it will have to be preached and taught in the church. Pastors will need to faithfully teach about virtue and vice, shepherds challenging their own congregation to be virtuous.

When we read the word *industrious* in the Old Testament, the Hebrew term behind it (*harus*) is an adjective meaning "diligent, i.e. pertaining to being persistently industrious." The noun form speaks of an "industrious person, i.e. one who is persistent in working." If you consult Noah Webster's 1828 dictionary on *industrious*, you find, "Diligent in business or study; constantly, regularly or habitually occupied in business; assiduous; opposed to slothful and idle."

Laziness in the Hebrew (*remiyah*) means "deceit, treachery, i.e. the state or condition of causing something false to be believed as true (in word or action), and so mislead." Besides "lazy," the word is also translated "slackness," "slackening," "deceit," and "treachery." Webster's indicates, "Disinclined to action or exertion; naturally or habitually slothful; sluggish; indolent; averse to labor."

Read

Read Proverbs 12:11-12; 13:11; 15:19; 20:13; 21:25-26; 24:30-34; 28:19.

What are the characteristics and corresponding rewards of industriousness?

What are the characteristics and corresponding "rewards" of laziness?

THRIFT VERSUS WASTE

Here's a rarely heard term in today's vocabulary: thrift. We need to relearn this word. It's the opposite of waste, useless consumption, or expenditure.

One of the ironies of our time is that some churches are preaching a message that leads to poverty rather than preaching the truth that leads to flourishing. Prosperity-gospel teaching does not result in prosperity; rather, it results in more poverty. The "health and wealth" gospel is animism and magic with a thin veneer of pious-sounding talk: "If you do this, God will bless you." This is prosperity via attempted "magic," seeking to manipulate God by invoking some kind of formula that requires Him to grant your request. Pastors should be speaking about thrift, about working hard and saving. The Bible teaches the benefits of hard work and saving.

My (Darrow) wife travels to Honduras every year. She serves in two very poor communities, El Triunfo and Las Chacaras, near the Nicaraguan border. Part of her work is to change culture. When she asks a group, "How many of you have a savings account?" they routinely say, "We cannot save, we are too poor." Last year she asked the people in these poor communities, "How many of you drink soda?" They all answered in the affirmative.

"And how much do you pay for these soft drinks?" They gave her an estimate.

She went on: "How many days a week do you have soft drinks? Multiply that by fifty-two weeks a year." The average family was spending $300–400 every year on soft drinks. Yet in these communities, many children were not in school because school cost $80 per year. The money spent on soft drinks would keep three or four children in school. This is not rocket science; this is wisdom.

This message will not necessarily come from the government. It comes from the Bible. Those of us who teach the Bible or preach need to teach virtues that lead to the prospering of nations.

When you work hard and you save, you create wealth. Wealth doesn't come from minerals in the ground, a credit card, a government check, or winning the lottery. Wealth is the product of human creativity and imagination; it is the result of hard work and saving.

Here is the definition of *thrift* from Webster's 1828 dictionary: "Frugality; good husbandry; economical management in regard to property. 1. Prosperity; success and advance in the acquisition of property; increase of worldly goods; gain. . . . 2. Vigorous growth, as of a plant." Note that the word *thrift* is derived from the word *thrive*. It is related to the concept of good husbandry (the care and cultivation of animals and crops, or management of resources).

The opposite of thrift is waste. The definition of this term, from the same dictionary, includes "to destroy wantonly or luxuriously; to squander; to cause to be lost through wantonness or negligence. Careless people waste their fuel, their food or their property. Children waste their inheritance."

Reflect

Are modern economies built on saving or consuming?

What do credit cards encourage? Explain your answer.

Do you tithe? Do you save?

What percentage of your income do you save every month?

What superfluous things could you cut back on to increase your savings?

My father taught me an order of priority for using the proceeds of my work:

- 10 percent tithe—to God and to charity
- 10 percent long-term savings
- enough short-term savings to survive a catastrophic event
- fixed expenses (food, clothing, housing, transportation, etc.)
- discretionary spending (entertainment, sports, etc.)

This practical application of thrift enables us to provide for ourselves, share with others in need, and have capital to invest in other people and their dreams. To live in wisdom means to gain and use wealth morally.

GENEROSITY VERSUS GREED

The final virtue from Proverbs that drives wealth creation may seem unlikely.

> ### Read
>
> Read Proverbs 21:5-8; 26:13-16; 28:19-22; 10:1-5; 21:17; 24:30-34.
>
> What do these passages reveal about the need for delayed gratification?
>
> What do these passages reveal about thrift and wealth creation?

It is somewhat counterintuitive to consider that giving money away is a good way to meet your own needs. But that's one of the principles Proverbs teaches. We see this, for example, in Proverbs 19:17: "Whoever is generous to the poor lends to the LORD, and he will repay him for his deed." Also, consider Proverbs 28:8: "Whoever multiplies his wealth by interest and profit gathers it for him who is generous to the poor."

God Himself is a generous giver. At the creation He provided a lavish home for humans, replete with everything the first couple and their generations of children could need or want. Thus, to be generous is to be like God.

A generous person is happy and joyful. We have nothing of our own; we are stewards of the possessions of Another. An attitude of thankfulness and generosity fits the one who understands this principle of stewardship.

In contrast, many societies promote selfishness and individual greed. We acquire in order to consume; we want things for ourselves. The culture says, "You deserve this!" as opposed to the Bible that says God blesses us so that we can bless others.

Greed is the opposite of generosity. Proverbs 7:20 warns that "death and destruction are never satisfied and neither are human eyes." Prosperity teaching reinforces greed. In the guise of biblical instruction, a vice is promoted. This message, so prevalent in many cultures of the world, including the churches in those cultures, is antithetical to the principles of Proverbs, which teach virtue. It is the responsibility of pastors and church leaders to teach the truths of Proverbs, including the virtue of generosity.

A greedy person ends up alone and in poverty of relationships. When you keep everything for yourself, you don't have open hands to receive anything from God. God gives more days to the generous person.

Many people believe the lie that they can't afford to give. Jesus corrects that idea when He speaks about the widow's offering. Jesus looked up and saw the rich putting their gifts into the offering box, and He saw a poor widow add two small copper coins. He then said, "Truly, I tell you, this poor widow has put in more than all of them. For they all contributed out of their abundance, but she out of her poverty put in all she had to live on" (Luke 21:3–4).

Not only the wealthy are called to generosity. All are stewards. Creation principles are universal in their application; even people who are poor can find blessing when they give with a generous spirit.

Reflect

When a person or family works hard and saves, what is the result?

What is to be done with the capital?

Our English word *generous* translates a Hebrew term (*nadib*) that means "willing, i.e. pertaining to being voluntary and uncoerced, implying generosity. The word is a derivative of the word for a leader, ruler, official, prince, i.e. one who is of great or noble status."

Webster's 1828 dictionary notes that the word generosity comes from the Latin, "generositas, from genus, race, kind, with reference to birth, blood, family. . . . The quality of being generous; liberality in principle; a disposition to give liberally or to bestow favors; a quality of the heart or mind opposed to meanness or parsimony."

Greed is the translation of the Hebrew word (*batsa*) meaning "cut off," that is, a figurative extension of to die or be dead; be greedy, to have a strong desire to make unjust gain. Webster defines greed as "having a keen desire of anything; eager to obtain; as greedy of gain."

Reflect

The Hebrew word for "generosity" means *"voluntary* giving." What is the difference between a free society where citizens give freely to help their neighbors and a coercive society where the government taxes people to help others?

What percentage of your income do you give every month?

What superfluous things could you cut back on to increase your generosity?

We live in consumer societies. How does consumer culture work against personal and national thriving?

Is God more interested in the development of your character or your accumulation of material wealth?

Make a personal list of things that you can and will do to flourish.

List some of the things that you are doing now that cause you to "wither" and "perish."

In summary, virtue leads to the creation of wealth. Vice leads to the stealing of wealth. How much wisdom is bound up in these simple statements? How much blessing—*shalom*—could be imparted to a society if such wisdom were honored?

Conclusion

Restoring Wisdom

We live in a world of depressing brokenness. This is reflected in poverty, disease, moral breakdown, and injustice of all kinds. Such are not God's intentions for the human family. Rather, they are the result of mankind's rebellion against God, His creation, and the ordinances that govern creation.

God's good intentions are for human flourishing in all areas of life (physical, social, economic, and political) and in all human relationships (personal, familial, communal, and national). When we fight against disease, moral breakdown, and injustice, we are joining God in His original creational intentions.

Stewarding the earth—another way to speak of sustaining the universe—is a shared responsibility. The sovereign God rules over all. He governs with divine providence through creation ordinances. But human beings are given responsibility from God. While God governs through His laws and ordinances, human beings govern through wisdom—that is, through obedience to God's creation mandate. We have been made to govern. We see this in the cultural mandate of Genesis 1:26–27. In Genesis 1:28 God blesses us, equips us, and empowers us for that task.

Folly abandons our God-given call to govern. How foolish we are when we try to live outside God's laws and ordinances. Folly abandons internal self-governance for a life of license and lawlessness. These behaviors lead to poverty and human languishing.

Why are people and nations poor and enslaved? The world gives many answers to this question and spends billions upon billions of dollars on poverty programs. Could one of the roots of poverty be that either we have forgotten the word *wisdom* or we ignore it? Could it be that as individuals and nations we make foolish decisions that lead to poverty?

Wisdom allows us to govern within the frame of ordinances of creation. This leads to human flourishing. The book of Proverbs is God's provision for human governance on a personal level (internal self-governance) and for the magistrates at a national level to move people and societies toward human flourishing. Let's restore the presence of wisdom in our vocabulary, in our decisions, and in our lives.

Let's end our journey together with a final creative reflection.

Reflect

What have you learned from this study of wisdom and flourishing?

What *Aha!* moments did you have while reading this book?

Develop a creative reflection that expresses what you have learned. Here are some ideas:
- Write a poem or song.
- Write a letter to God confessing any foolishness you have found in your life and asking Him to give you a heart and a spirit for wisdom.
- Choreograph a dance.
- Paint a picture.
- Write a monologue.

Endnotes

1. In this book we will often use the term *man* in the classical sense of human beings in general or the human race. In this sense "man" includes both women and men.

2. The following give further insights into God's provision of food for man:

   You cause the grass to grow for the livestock
       and plants for man to cultivate,
   that he may bring forth food from the earth
       and wine to gladden the heart of man,
   oil to make his face shine
       and bread to strengthen man's heart. (Ps. 104:14–15)
   He who gives food to all flesh,
       for his steadfast love endures forever. (Ps. 136:25)
   The eyes of all look to you,
       and you give them their food in due season.
   You open your hand;
       you satisfy the desire of every living thing. (Ps. 145:15–16)
   Some will depart from the faith by devoting themselves to deceitful spirits and teachings of demons, through the insincerity of liars . . . who forbid marriage and require abstinence from foods that God created to be received with thanksgiving by those who believe and know the truth. For everything created by God is good, and nothing is to be rejected if it is received with thanksgiving. (1 Tim. 4:1–4)

3. "v.i. flur'ish. [L. floresco, from floreo. The primary sense is to open, expand, enlarge, or to shoot out, as in glory, L. ploro.] 1. To thrive; to grow luxuriantly; to increase and enlarge, as a healthy, growing plant. 2. To be prosperous; to increase in wealth or honor." Unless otherwise noted, all English dictionary definitions are from Webster's 1828 *American Dictionary of the English Language*.

4. "I.e., have a plant be in a state of growth and maturity that can include the budding and blossoming of the fruit buds or flowers. Note: In some contexts, this refers to prosperity or a favorable state or circumstance." Unless otherwise noted, all Hebrew lexicon entries are from the J. Swanson, *Dictionary of Biblical Languages with Semantic Domains: Hebrew (Old Testament)*, electronic ed. (Oak Harbor, WA: Logos Research Systems, 1997).

5. Thomas Cahill, *The Gifts of the Jews: How a Tribe of Desert Nomads Changed the Way Everyone Thinks and Feels* (New York: Anchor Books, 1998), series page.

6. Cahill, *Gifts of the Jews*, 239–40.

7. Cahill, *Gifts of the Jews*, 240–41.

8. Os Guinness, *A Free People's Suicide: Sustainable Freedom and the American Future* (Downers Grove, IL: InterVarsity Press, 2012), 114.

9. Christian Overman, *The Lost Purpose for Learning: An Essay on United States Education with Implications for All Nations* (Bellevue, WA: Ablaze Publishing, 2016), 29.

10. Guinness, *Free People's Suicide*, 102.

11. Guinness, *Free People's Suicide*, 106. Guinness's book comprises a wealth of related insights into these subjects.

12. E. L. Youmans, *The Noah Plan History and Geography Curriculum Guide* (Chesapeake, VA: The Foundation for American Christian Education, 1998), 68.

13. J. R. R. Tolkien, *Tree and Leaf* (London: Unwin Books, 1964), 68.

14. An observation made by C. S. Lewis in *Mere Christianity* (New York: HarperCollins, 1980), 136.

15. For further reading on the power of the creation story as it relates to human development, see Darrow L. Miller with Stan Guthrie, *Discipling Nations: The Power of Truth to Transform Cultures*, 3rd ed. (Seattle: YWAM Publishing, 2018).

16. There is documentary film about this project; see "Landfill Harmonic," Vimeo, September 7, 2016, http://vimeo.com/52711779.

17. The stories here are used by permission.

18. Noah Webster, *American Dictionary of the English Language* (1828). Available online at http://webstersdictionary1828.com/. When the United States was founded, lexicographer and the "father of American education" Noah Webster produced this dictionary, consciously developed from the framework of a biblical worldview. This is the American Dictionary of the English Language, not the English Dictionary of the English Language. Webster understood that founding a free nation like the United States would require a dictionary consciously reflecting the language of freedom born out of Judeo-Christian theism. In her paper "The Remarkable Role of the Bible in Early American Education" (available at http://www.disciplenations.org/papers-articles-videos/), Dr. Elizabeth Youmans points out that the development of this work "required the mastery of 26 languages. In addition to researching the root meanings of words, he also researched words in the Hebrew and Greek lexicons and defined them according to how they were used in Scripture. . . . *Webster's 1828 is the only dictionary in the world that includes biblical meanings of words.*" Further references to Webster's dictionary come from this source.

19. Elizabeth L. Youmans, Jill C. Thrift, and Scott D. Allen, *As the Family Goes, So Goes the Nation: Principles and Practices for Building Healthy Families* (Orlando: Chrysalis International; Phoenix: Disciple Nations Alliance, 2013), 61.

20. Thomas Dubay, *The Evidential Power of Beauty: Science and Theology Meet* (San Francisco: Ignatius Press, 1999), 50.

21. Dubay, *Evidential Power of Beauty*, 43.

22. We have written elsewhere about the characteristics of nations that encourage wealth development. See Darrow L. Miller, *Rethinking Social Justice: Restoring Biblical Compassion* (Seattle: YWAM Publishing, 2015).

23. David Hill Scott, "A Vision of *Veritas*: What Christian Scholarship Can

Learn from the Puritan's 'Technology' of Integrating Truth," accessed November 11, 2016, http://www.leaderu.com/aip/docs/scott.html.

24. Scott, "Vision of *Veritas*." This three-book paradigm was originated by seventeenth-century Czech Moravian educational reformer John Comenius.

25. Related to Darrow by Jun Vencer's colleague, Roy Wingerd, at the DNA Forum in Phoenix, Arizona, on April 16, 2002.

26. He goes on to point out that "these tendencies or determinations, whether called laws or affections of matter, have been established by the Creator, and are, with a peculiar felicity of expression, denominated in Scripture, ordinances of heaven."

27. Thomas Cahill, *The Gifts of the Jews: How a Tribe of Desert Nomads Changed the Way Everyone Thinks and Feels* (New York: Anchor Books, 1998), 239.

28. With reference to "metaphysical," Webster notes the following: "The natural division of things that exist is into body and mind, things material and immaterial. The former belong to physics, and the latter to the science of metaphysics."

29. For more on this, see Darrow L. Miller, *Discipling Nations: The Power of Truth to Transform Culture*, 3rd ed. (Seattle: YWAM Publishing, 2018).

30. Dr. Todd Miles, associate professor of Theology, Western Seminary, THS 501 class notes.

31. R. P. McCabe, "Science and the Origins of Life," *Doctrine and Life*, 131. Quoted in Thomas Dubay, *The Evidential Power of Beauty: Science and Theology Meet* (San Francisco: Ignatius Press, 1999), 216.

32. Dubay, *Evidential Power of Beauty*, 201.

33. An exception is sea birds, who swim underwater in short bursts notwithstanding.

34. Robert Sadler with Marie Chapian, *The Emancipation of Robert Sadler: The Powerful True Story of a Twentieth-Century Plantation Slave* (Minneapolis: Bethany House, 2012), 30.

35. E. Stanley Jones, *The Unshakable Kingdom and the Unchanging Person* (Nashville: Abingdon, 1972), 54.

36. Without mounting a complete treatment here, we would simply note that no one can live consistently with a Hindu mindset that denies the reality of an objective creation. Paul's words apply here: "For what can be known about God is plain to them, because God has shown it to them. For his invisible attributes, namely, his eternal power and divine nature, have been clearly perceived, ever since the creation of the world, in the things that have been made. So they are without excuse" (Rom. 1:19–20).

37. "The true and genuine method of philosophizing is to draw all conclusions from Scripture, reason and sense." Quoted and translated from Latin by Rand, "Liberal Education in Seventeenth-Century Harvard," 539. See David Hill Scott, "A Vision of *Veritas*: What Christian Scholarship Can Learn from the Puritan's 'Technology' of Integrating Truth," note 29, accessed November 11, 2016, http://www.leaderu.com/aip/docs/scott.html#text29.

38. Georgia Purdom, "Harvard: No Longer 'Truth for Christ and the Church,'" Answers in Genesis, October 11, 2011, http://blogs.answersingenesis.org/blogs/

georgia-purdom/2011/10/11/harvard-no-longer-truth-for-christ-and-the-church.

39. See Ps. 89:11; 115:16; Col. 1:17; Heb. 1:3.

40. Wilbur F. Tillett, "Providence," in *The International Standard Bible Encyclopedia* (Wilmington, DE: Associated Publishers and Authors, 1915), 4:2484.

41. Ken Hopper and Will Hopper, *The Puritan Gift: Reclaiming the American Dream Amidst Global Financial Chaos* (London: I. B. Tauris, 2009), 15–18.

42. It bears noting that everything God does is supernatural because He is transcendent; He dwells above and beyond the universe. Here we mean "supernatural" as we normally think of it, i.e., an act of God that is obviously outside the norms we are accustomed to.

43. The technical definition of this law is "Every process occurring in nature proceeds in the sense in which the sum of the entropies of all bodies taking part in the process is increased." Quoted in Andreas Greven, Gerhard Keller, and Gerald Warnecke, eds., *Entropy* (Princeton: Princeton University Press, 2014), 131.

44. Actually, it may be more accurate to identify this as a postcreation law, something that came with the cosmic reversal.

45. "In the second half of the fourth century, three theologians from the province of Cappadocia [in modern-day Turkey] had a profound influence upon the character of Christian theology. There were Basil of Caesarea, his brother Gregory of Nyssa, and Basil's close friend Gregory of Nazianzus. They gave final shape to the Greek doctrine of the Trinity and through their efforts Arianism was finally defeated." *The New International Dictionary of the Christian Church*, ed. J. D. Douglas (Grand Rapids: Zondervan, 1978), 191.

46. The term comes from the combination of two Greek words, *peri* (around) and *chorea* (dance).

47. Timothy Keller, *The Reason for God: Belief in an Age of Skepticism* (New York: Riverhead Books, 2008), 224.

48. C. S. Lewis, *Perelandra* (New York: Macmillan, 1944), 217.

49. Greg Uttinger, "The Theology of the Ancient Creeds Part 4: The Athanasian Creed," Chalcedon, August 27, 2002, http://chalcedon.edu/research/articles/the-theology-of-the-ancient-creeds-part-4-the-athanasian-creed/.

50. K. Alan Snyder, *If the Foundations Are Destroyed: Biblical Principles and Civil Government* (Marion, IN: Principle Press, 1994), 34–35.

51. "From John Adams to Massachusetts Militia, 11 October 1798," Founders Online, accessed August 9, 2018, https://founders.archives.gov/documents/Adams/99-02-02-3102.

52. Don Hawkinson, *Character for Life: An American Heritage* (Green Forest, AR: New Leaf Press, 2005), 24.

53. Elizabeth L. Youmans, "The Christian Principle of Self Government," AMO® *Apprenticeship Manual* (Orlando: Chrysalis International, 2010), 127.

54. "Letter to a Member of the National Assembly," 1791, accessed August 9, 2018, https://www.bartleby.com/73/1051.html.

55. "Speech to the Massachusetts Bible Society" (1849), quoted in *Robert Winthrop, Addresses and Speeches on Various Occasions* (Little, Brown, 1852), 172, accessed September 25, 2017, https://en.wikiquote.org/wiki/Robert_Charles_Winthrop.

56. "Saying published anonymously in *The Dayspring*, Vol. 10 (1881) by the Unitarian Sunday-School Society, and quoted in *Life and Labor* (1887) by Smiles; this is most often attributed to George Dana Boardman, at least as early as 1884, but also sometimes attributed to William Makepeace Thackeray as early as 1891, probably because in *Life and Labor* Smiles adds a quote by Thackeray right after this one, to Charles Reade in 1903, and to William James as early as 1906, because it appears in his *Principles of Psychology* (1890)." "Samuel Smiles," accessed September 25, 2017, https://en.wikiquote.org/wiki/Samuel_Smiles.

57. "Heart Problems: The Looting in Iraq Illustrates the Moral and Political Crisis That Plagues the Islamic World," *World*, May 3, 2003, https://world.wng.org/2003/05/heart_problems.

58. "Making Waves," *Tabletalk* from Ligonier Ministries and R. C. Sproul, January 2001, 12.

59. Personal conversation between Darrow Miller and a Russian Christian in the 1980s.

60. David Hill Scott, "A Vision of *Veritas*: What Christian Scholarship Can Learn from the Puritan's 'Technology' of Integrating Truth," accessed November 22, 2016, http://www.leaderu.com/aip/docs/scott.html.

61. Another term for the creation mandate.

62. There is more than one school of thought about what comprises the Wisdom literature. Some authorities also include Song of Songs and some of the Psalms, James, etc.

63. Western Seminary BLS501 course lecture, spring 2011.

64. R. Laird Harris, Gleason L. Archer Jr., and Bruce K. Waltke, *The Theological Wordbook of the Old Testament* (Chicago: Moody Press, 1980), accessed in BibleWorks, copyright © 1992–2008 BibleWorks, LLC. The quote is from A. S. Herbert, which is contained in the following entry for *mashal*: "Proverb, parable, allegory, byword, taunt, discourse. Of great interest is the wide number of translations for this word in most English translations of the Old Testament. . . . To translate mashal simply as 'proverb' misses the wide sweep of the word, suggested by the many suggested translations. We are accustomed to think of a proverb as a short, pithy, epigrammatic saying which assumes the status of gnomic truth. In the Old Testament, however, the word mashal may be synonymous with an extended parable. . . . It may refer to an extended didactic discourse (Pro. 1:8–19 for example). . . . A. S. Herbert has well stated that in the Old Testament the 'proverb'/ mashal had 'a clearly recognizable purpose: that of quickening an apprehension of the real as distinct from the wished for ... of compelling the hearer or reader to form a judgment on himself, his situation or his conduct.' (Herbert, 196)."

65. "Judaism's Sexual Revolution: Why Judaism (and then Christianity) Rejected Homosexuality," http://www.orthodoxytoday.org/articles2/PragerHomosexuality.php.

66. "A Little Scandal Never Hurt Anyone," Little Light Studios, November 20, 2013, http://www.littlelightstudios.tv/little-scandal-never-hurt-one/.

67. Emaleigh Grantz, "Rap Music: Does It Promote a Rape Culture?," Prezi, April 18, 2014, https://prezi.com/xdpblftain_b/rap-music-does-it-promote-a-rape-culture/.

68. Katie McDonough, "Richard Dawkins Defends 'Mild Pedophilia,' Says It Does Not Cause 'Lasting Harm,'" *Salon*, September 10, 2013, http://www.salon.com/2013/09/10/richard_dawkins_defends_mild_pedophilia_says_it_does_not_cause_lasting_harm/.

69. Charlotte Gill, "Disgusted By Incest? Genetic Sexual Attraction Is Real and On the Rise," *The Telegraph*, September 9, 2016, http://www.telegraph.co.uk/women/family/disgusted-by-incest-genetic-sexual-attraction-is-real-and-on-the/.

70. Brendan O'Neill, "Ian McEwan Notes That 2 + 2 = 4 — Horrified, the LGBT Orwellians Make Him Take It Back," *National Review*, April 11, 2016, http://www.nationalreview.com/article/433896/trans-activists-identity-politics-ian-mcewan-lgbt-orwellian-1984.

71. Matt Blake, "Bestiality Brothels Are 'Spreading Through Germany' Warns Campaigner as Abusers Turn to Sex with Animals as 'Lifestyle Choice,'" *Daily Mail*, July 1, 2013, http://www.dailymail.co.uk/news/article-2352779/Bestiality-brothels-spreading-Germany-campaigner-claims-abusers-sex-animals-lifestyle-choice.html.

72. Here are the entries for these three terms from one leading lexicon (R. Laird Harris, Gleason L. Archer Jr., and Bruce K. Waltke, *The Theological Wordbook of the Old Testament* [Chicago: Moody Press, 1980]).

    Knowledge: While ordinarily gained by experience, knowledge is also the contemplative perception possessed by the wise man (Pro. 1:4; Pro. 2:6; Pro. 5:2; Ecc. 1:18). In addition to knowledge of secular matters yada is also used of one's relation to the divine. The related word *da'at* is a general term for knowledge, particularly that which is of a personal, experimental nature (Pro. 24:5). It is also used for technical knowledge or ability. It appears parallel with wisdom and understanding, instruction, and law. Da'at is the contemplative perception of the wise man (Pro. 1:4; Pro. 2:6; Pro. 5:2; Ecc. 1:18). The word is also used for moral cognition.

    Understanding: Yada generally describes the process whereby one gains knowledge through experience with objects and circumstances. Ben is a power of judgment and perceptive insight and is demonstrated in the use of knowledge. Its main English usage is "understanding" or "insight."

    Wisdom: The usages of *hokma* cover the whole gamut of human experience. Wisdom is seen in the skill of technical work in making garments for the high priest (Exo. 28:3), craftsmanship in metal work (Exo. 31:3, 6), as well as the execution of battle tactics (Isa. 10:13). Wisdom is required from government leaders and heads of state for administration (Deu. 34:9; 2 Sam. 14:20), including pagan leaders as well as Israelites (Eze. 28:2-5). Prudence, an aspect of wisdom, is expressed by those who speak with wisdom (Psa. 37:30; Pro. 10:31), and who use time carefully (Psa. 90:12). This kind of wisdom in the practical affairs of life is derived from the revelation of God (Isa. 33:6). The source of all wisdom is a personal God who is holy, righteous, and just. His wisdom is expressed against the background of His omnipotence and omniscience. By His wisdom God numbered the clouds (Job 38:37), founded the earth (Pro. 3:19), and made the world (Jer 10:12). Wisdom, being found in God, is regarded as a divine attribute (Job 12:13). He alone knows wisdom in its truest sense (Job 28:20, 23). The wisdom of God is not found in man's speculation. He alone must provide this wisdom for man's guidance so that man can live the best possible moral and ethical life (Pro. 2:6; Job 11:6). Wisdom for man is not only to make one humanly wise, but also to lead him to fear the Lord, for this is the beginning of all wisdom (Job 28:28). True wisdom for man involves knowing the Holy One.

73. The creation mandate and the cultural mandate are two ways to speak of the same truth. One emphasizes the timing of the commission (given at the creation), the other emphasizes the nature of the commission (to create godly culture).

74. C. S. Lewis, "Transposition," in *The Weight of Glory and Other Addresses* (New York: Macmillan, 1949), 71.

75. E. J. Schnabel, "Wisdom," in *New Dictionary of Biblical Theology*, ed. T. Desmond Alexander and Brian S. Rosner (Downers Grove, IL: InterVarsity Press, 2000), 845.

76. The Hebrew word is defined as follows:

yirâ. When God is the object of fear, the emphasis is again upon awe or reverence. This attitude of reverence is the basis for real wisdom (Job 28:28; Psa 111:10; Prov 9:10; Prov 15:33). Indeed, the phrase sets the theme for the book of Proverbs. it is used in Prov 1:7; recurs in Prov 9:10 and twelve other verses. The fear of the Lord is to hate evil (Prov 8:13), is a fountain of life (Prov 14:27), it tendeth to life (Prov 19:23), and prolongeth days (Prov 10:27). Numerous passages relate this fear of God to piety and righteous living: it motivates faithful living (Jer 32:40). Fear of God results in caring for strangers (Gen 20:11). Just rule is rule in the fear of God (2 Sam 23:3). Fear of the Almighty does not withhold kindness from friends (Job 6:14). Economic abuses against fellow Jews were contrary to the fear of God (Neh 5:9). The fear of the Lord turns men from evil (Prov 16:6). (R. Laird Harris, Gleason L. Archer Jr., and Bruce K. Waltke, *The Theological Wordbook of the Old Testament* [Chicago: Moody Press, 1980]).

77. AMO is an acronym for "Feed My Lambs" in the Romance languages (Apascenta Minhas Ovelhas, Apacienta Mis Ovejas). The verb *amo* means "I love." See https://www.amoprogram.com.

78. Susan T. Foh, *Women and the Word of God* (Phillipsburg, NJ: Presbyterian & Reformed, 1978), 156–57.

79. A paraphrase version of the Bible, THE MESSAGE, personifies folly as "Madame Whore" in Proverbs 9:13. Much of Proverbs is addressed to the young man, tempted by prostitutes. This graphic label for folly—Madam Whore—powerfully captures the allure and danger of choosing foolishness over wisdom.

80. Mark Buchanan, *The Rest of God: Restoring Your Soul by Restoring Sabbath* (Nashville: Thomas Nelson, 2007), 40.

81. "Prolepsis," *Encyclopedia Britannica*, accessed September 11, 2017, https://www.britannica.com/topic/prolepsis-literature.

82. *Webster's Seventh New Collegiate Dictionary* (Springfield, MA: G & C Merriam, 1970), 681.

83. E. Stanley Jones, *The Word Became Flesh* (Nashville: Abingdon, 1963), Week 7, Tuesday.

84. Jacques Monod, *Chance and Necessity* (New York: Alfred A. Knopf, 1971), 21–22.

85. Letter to Messrs., the Abbes Chalut, and Arnaud, 17 April 1787. Quoted in Alan Snyder, "Benjamin Franklin," *Pondering Principles* (blog), accessed November 22, 2016, http://ponderingprinciples.com/quotes/franklin/.

86. It's also worthy of note that if God saw fit to include this verse in the Bible, that tells us something about His priority for a full-life growth and development in individual men and women.

87. Theologians use the term *hypostatic union* to capture the scriptural teaching that Jesus Christ was fully God and fully man. He was 100 percent divine and 100 percent human (not 50–50), and yet He was one person.

88. Dr. Vencer's teachings bear similarity to those of the Disciple Nations Alliance with one difference. The DNA seeks to influence the grass roots of society, while Vencer's material is directed to the "grass tops," i.e., society's leaders.

89. G. K. Chesterton, *A Short History of England* (London: Chatto and Windus, 1917), 124.

90. *Louw-Nida Greek-English Lexicon of the New Testament Based on Semantic Domains*, 2nd ed., ed. J. P. Louw and E. A. Nida (New York: United Bible Societies, 1988).

91. Vishal Mangalwadi, "Enron, Corruption and True Spirituality," accessed September 12, 2017, http://listserv.virtueonline.org/pipermail/virtueonline_listserv.virtueonline.org/2002-February/003275.html.

92. C. S. Lewis, *Mere Christianity* (New York: HarperCollins, 1980), 122.

93. The germ of this insight came from Timothy Keller.

94. Joe Rigney, *The Things of Earth* (Wheaton, IL: Crossway, 2015), 71.

95. Mayo Clinic Staff, "Forgiveness: Letting Go of Grudges and Bitterness," November 4, 2017, http://www.mayoclinic.org/healthy-lifestyle/adult-health/in-depth/forgiveness/art-20047692.

96. Swanson, *Dictionary of Biblical Languages*.

97. Laura Ingalls Wilder, *Little Town on the Prairie* (New York: Harper & Row, 1970), 76–77.

98. One of the greatest causes of poverty in the world is a lie—men are superior to women. Women and wives are objectivized and sexualized by cultures all over the world. They are stripped of their dignity. The book of Proverbs gives specific instructions on how to remedy this, restoring the God-given dignity of women.

99. Darrow L. Miller, *Nurturing the Nations: Reclaiming the Dignity of Women in Building Healthy Cultures* (Colorado Springs: Paternoster, 2007).

100. The following list is adapted from a class discussion at Youth With A Mission (JUCUM) in Junos, Puerto Rico, November 4–8, 2013.

101. The language reflects the creation order, that is, God made male (husband) and female (wife). But the terminology must not be allowed to obscure a clear scriptural reflection: God calls some people to singleness, a state that is even preferable to marriage in some ways (see 1 Cor. 7:32–35), and some to marriage. Only the Christian religion affirms this truth.

102. The Hebrew word used throughout Proverbs and often translated "son" is *ben*. Its meaning is broader than merely a male child. It can mean "child, i.e., the immediate offspring of a parent, either male or female . . . offspring . . . grandchild . . . descendent." J. Swanson, *Dictionary of Biblical Languages with Semantic Domains: Hebrew (Old Testament)* (Oak Harbor, WA: Logos Research Systems, 1997).

103. Here's an important reminder of something we have noted elsewhere. For the most part, the material in Proverbs is not composed of promises. Rather, Wisdom literature is composed of general observations. Generally speaking, wise and godly parents will produce children who are godly. The exceptions to that principle do not compromise the integrity of Proverbs, since these are general principles rather than promises.

104. Janie B. Cheaney, "Broken Music," *World*, November 16, 2013, accessed November 26, 2017, https://world.wng.org/2013/11/broken_music.

105. Cheaney, "Broken Music."

106. Note that Eph. 5:22, "Wives, submit to your own husbands, as to the Lord," is immediately preceded by the mutual command "submitting to one another out of reverence for Christ."

107. Rabbi Daniel Lapin, *Thou Shalt Prosper* (Hoboken, NJ: John Wiley & Sons, 2010), 60–61.

108. C. S. Lewis, *The Four Loves* (New York: Harcourt Brace Jovanovich, 1960), 92.

109. These themes are unpacked in Dr. Gonzales's 2014 book, *Machismo and Matriarchy: Toxic Roots that Blight the Latin American Culture* (Chesapeake, VA: Semilla), available at www.semilla.org.

110. Gonzales, *Machismo and Matriarchy*, 14.

111. For more on this, see appendix A in *Rethinking Social Justice: Restoring Biblical Compassion* (Seattle: YWAM Publishing, 2015).

112. Abraham Rabinovich, "Egyptian President Calls for 'Religious Revolution' in Islam," *Washington Free Beacon*, January 4, 2015, http://freebeacon.com/nation al-security/egyptian-president-calls-for-religious-revolution-in-islam/#sthash .DWgB0e1y.dpuf.

113. C. S. Lewis, *The Abolition of Man* (New York: Touchstone, 1996), 37.

114. *Oxford Universal English Dictionary* (Oxford: Oxford University Press, 1937), 7:1583.

115. In his book *The Other Path*, Hernando Desoto critiques the nonformal economy in his country of Peru. He established the Institute for Liberty and Democracy and sent staff to find out what it would take to set up a two-sewing-machine factory. To open such a shop legally, without paying bribes, required a financial outlay (in costs and fees) of $1,231 (the equivalent of thirty-two months ofat the minimum

wage). The cost in time was 289 days at six hours a day. Over the course of 289 days, ten bribes were solicited. Desoto said out of this experience, "I now know why some countries are poor and others are rich. We're a world of 169 countries, and only about 25 of them have 'made it' economically. They were able to do so because they stripped governments of the power to deprive the humblest citizens of the fruits of their industry and creativity."

116. William Blackstone, *Commentaries*, quoted in Vierna M. Hall, comp. *The Christian History of the Constitution of the United States* of America: Christian Self-Government (San Francisco: Foundation For American Christian Education, 1966), 142.

117. Robert Frank, "Don't Envy the Super-Rich, They Are Miserable," *Wall Street Journal*, March 9, 2011, https://blogs.wsj.com/wealth/2011/03/09/dont-envy-the-super-rich-they-are-miserable/.

118. The perceptive reader may recognize that Jesus uses the exact same phrase, "It is written," to affirm the authority of the Hebrew Scriptures. But Jesus's use of the phrase is different than Islam's. Jesus is referencing a passage of Scripture. Islam uses the phrase to indicate something in the Koran that is inviolable.

119. "How People Who Live on Less Than Two Dollars a Day Taught Me to Redefine Poverty," March 31, 2014, http://blog.tifwe.org/redefining-poverty/.

Equipping the Church to Transform the World

The Disciple Nations Alliance is a global network of individuals, churches and organizations with a common vision: to see the global Church rise to her full potential as God's instrument for the healing, blessing, and transformation of the nations.

The Disciple Nations Alliance was founded in 1997 through a partnership between Food for the Hungry (www.fh.org) and Harvest (www.harvest foundation.org). Our mission is to influence the paradigm and practice of local churches around the world, helping them recognize and abandon false beliefs and embrace a robust biblical worldview—bringing truth, justice, and beauty into every sphere of society; and to demonstrate Christ's love in practical ways, addressing the brokenness in their communities and nations beginning with their own resources.

For more information and a host of resources, curricula, books, study materials, and application tools, please visit www.disciplenations.org or contact us at info@disciplenations.org.

About the Authors

Darrow L. Miller is an author, lecturer, and cofounder of the Disciple Nations Alliance. For twenty-seven years Darrow served with Food for the Hungry International, a relief and development organization of Christian motivation working to feed both the physical and spiritual hungers of people in developing countries on four continents. For nearly thirty-five years, Darrow has been a popular speaker at conferences and seminars on topics that include worldview and development, culture and poverty, the dignity of women, the great commission, vocation and work, social justice, wholistic ministry, and the role of the church in development.

Two significant experiences shaped Darrow's vocational pursuits. The first occurred during a trip to Mexico at age nineteen, when he first encountered poverty. The second happened while studying under Francis Schaeffer at L'Abri Fellowship in Switzerland, where he learned that Christianity is objectively true; it is reality, even if no one believes it. These experiences motivated Darrow to devote his life to serving the poor and hungry from a thoroughly Christian worldview.

Before engaging in the fight against hunger and poverty in 1981, Darrow spent three years on staff at L'Abri Fellowship, three years as a student pastor at Northern Arizona University, and two years as pastor of an urban church in Denver, Colorado. In addition to earning his master's degree in higher adult education from Arizona State University, Darrow has pursued graduate studies in philosophy, theology, Christian apologetics, biblical studies, and missions in the United States, Israel, and Switzerland.

Darrow has traveled, studied, and worked in over one hundred countries. His books and articles have been translated, in whole or in part, into fourteen languages. Darrow blogs at *Darrow Miller and Friends* (darrowmillerand friends.com). He can be found on Facebook at https://www.facebook.com/DarrowMiller.

Darrow and his wife, Marilyn, reside in Phoenix, Arizona. They have four adult children and fourteen grandchildren.

Gary Brumbelow is the Disciple Nations Alliance editorial manager. He manages the blog *Darrow Miller and Friends* and serves as editor and co-writer on various book projects.

For eight years Gary served as a cross-cultural church planting missionary among First Nations people of Canada. His career also includes fourteen years as executive director of InterAct Ministries, an Oregon-based church-planting organization working in Canada, Alaska, and Siberia.

Gary is a graduate of Grace University and earned an MA from Wheaton College and a Graduate Studies Diploma from Western Seminary. He lives in a suburb of Portland, Oregon, with his wife, Valerie. They have two grown sons and twelve grandchildren.

In addition to his work with the DNA, Gary serves as the pastor of Troutdale Community Church.